AND THE WALLS BECAME
THE WORLD ALL AROUND

Johanna Ekström

Skiffer 1993

Vitöga 1994

Rachels hus 1995

Fiktiva dagboken 1997

Gå förlorad 1998

Vad vet jag om hållfasthet 2000

Jag ska vakna stående 2003

Avskedsstafetten 2004

Titta, hon kryper 2006

Det enda främmande 2008

Om man håller sig i solen 2012

Dagbok 1996–2002 2016

Meningarna 2020

Sigrid Rausing

History, Memory and Identity in Post-Soviet Estonia:
The End of a Collective Farm 2004

Everything is Wonderful 2014

Mayhem 2017

AND THE WALLS
BECAME THE WORLD
ALL AROUND

Johanna Ekström

Sigrid Rausing

Translated from the Swedish
by Sigrid Rausing

GRANTA

Granta Publications, 12 Addison Avenue, London W11 4QR
First published in Great Britain by Granta Books, 2024

Originally published in Swedish as *Och väggarna förvandlades till världen runtomkring* by Albert Bonniers Förlag, Stockholm, Sweden, 2023.

A CIP catalogue record for this book is available from the British Library.

1   3   5   7   9   10   8   6   4   2

ISBN 978 1 80351 156 6 (hardback)
ISBN 978 1 80351 158 0 (ebook)

Typeset in Garamond by Patty Rennie
Printed and bound by CPI Group (UK) Ltd, Croydon, CR0 4YY

www.granta.com

MIX
Paper | Supporting responsible forestry
FSC
www.fsc.org   FSC® C171272

I had the idea that the world's so full of pain
it must sometimes make a kind of singing.
And that sequence helps, as much as order helps—
First an ego, and then pain, and then the singing.

Robert Hass, 'Faint Music',
from *Sun Under Wood* (1996)

CONTENTS

INTRODUCTION

My closest friend, the Swedish writer Johanna Ekström, was diagnosed with melanoma of the eye in September 2021. By the following spring the cancer had metastasised to the liver, and her oncologist estimated that she had only two or three months to live.

She only survived for two weeks after the final prognosis. Unfathomable hours.

Johanna remained who she was – funny, realistic, and without a trace of self-pity. She would talk about her tumours almost with tenderness, holding her hand against her swollen liver as she talked, and I thought of her extraordinary capacity to give everything space. To not censor or deny whatever she, or we, wished did not exist.

We met when we were young (she was younger) and formed a friendship, an ongoing conversation shaped by language, reading, writing and psychoanalysis. When I think of her now, I realise that it's hard to describe a close friend because what one sees and thinks about is the feeling, the mood, the enduring microculture you generate together. Johanna was my closest friend, but she was also like a younger sister. Some sort of unspoken authority was vested in me, some sort of wild freedom in her. She would come to stay, and sooner or later, sometimes in the middle of a conversation, we would start moving furniture, the aesthetic she grew up with and rebelled against unleashed; her extraordinary strength and pace and energy contrasting with my own perennial lassitude.

As a writer, she was experimental and precise in equal measure. She played with words and syntax, but was rigorously attentive to her sentences. Perhaps the quest for the right position for a piece of furniture somehow mirrored her quest for the right word or phrase in a conversation or in a piece of text – a slight obsession, cloaked in irony and humour. An exercise of diminishing returns if one had an end in mind, but she – or we – never did. The quest itself was the thing, the process of continuous exploration. No right answers, only questions and observations.

Johanna was the child of writers, and the idea of the perfect articulation of interiors (in both senses) and text had shaped her since childhood. Her mother, Margareta Ekström, was a highly regarded short-story writer and translator. Her father, Per Wästberg, is a prolific writer and editor. He was President of International PEN, founded the Swedish section of Amnesty International, and was deeply involved in the anti-apartheid struggle. He recently stepped down from chairing the Swedish Academy's Nobel Prize in Literature committee. Per and Margareta (and Johanna and her younger brother Jakob) were the 1970s photogenic heart of literary Stockholm, living in an old house whose sparse yet functional interior reflected a cultural ideal of openness and liberation.

Johanna's quiet place of safety, by contrast (in this book at least) was her grandparents' farm kitchen, a gentle and timeless space. And she needed safety: she had turned seriously anorexic when she was very young, a dangerous state of mind her parents ignored in accordance with the prevalent advice of the day. Per and Margareta eventually separated, and Johanna made her way from anorexia via the disco scene into writing, debuting with a well-regarded collection of poetry aged twenty-two.

We met in 1990. Her parents and mine knew each other a little and following the separation Margareta had become a friend. She organised a celebration for my mother in Stockholm (they were the same age). Johanna, ever competent, endlessly energetic, had made the dinner for twenty or so people, with her then boyfriend. I had brought my old friend Mark, and we all instantly recognised some quality of irony and longing in each other, a faintly under-parented rebellion and hunger, though Johanna was already then set on a serious writing path.

A steady readership, a voice, a body of literary works. Johanna's writing voice was experimental, spare and exact. Her interior decoration, too, was experimental, spare and exact, but as exacting as she could be no one loved playing with shallow tropes more than Johanna. Something in that first meeting – the irony, the camp, the *gleefulness* – stayed with us forever. She had an affectionate, at times exasperated, regard for the eccentricities of her paternal relatives, a public-spirited and generous Jewish family intermarried with gifted others. Margareta, by contrast, had almost no family. Margareta's loneliness, her privacy, her gift, her height, her presence, her joy in a bunch of tulips (the right vase, the right place) were devastated by a catastrophic stroke brought on by excessive blood thinners for a heart condition. By the time she was found on the bathroom floor of her locked flat she had lost most of her capacity for speech and linguistic thinking.

But flowers and music and delicacies could still delight her.

Johanna, by that time, had already been through her first marriage, to Erik Pauser, a talented documentary film-maker and artist. They worked together for a while – Johanna was a visual artist as well as a writer and a well-known gallery had shown her work at several group and single exhibitions.

She later married the non-fiction writer and journalist Tomas Lappalainen, and they had a much-beloved daughter, T. The marriage eventually fell apart, and from then on they lived the one week on, one week off life of separated parents in Sweden – childcare is almost always shared equally there, and so it was in this case. Johanna lived in a small flat in Stockholm, and that's where a group of us looked after her in the last weeks of her life.

T is my goddaughter. D, my son, was Johanna's god-son.

Johanna's writing, long before this book, often included references to the metaphorical nature of seeing – to see or to be blind, to see or to deny what you see: 'I can never see clearly,' she wrote in her 1997 autobiographical novel *A Fictional Diary*. 'I am always blind in one eye, and I can't focus with the other. I don't want to force myself to see clearly. Who says that is how reality should be seen?'

It's hard to escape a sense of fate. The exquisitely articulate Margareta lost her language and Johanna, whose vision, and perception of what she saw, had always been extraordinarily clear and precise, lost most of the sight in her right eye after treatment for eye melanoma.

A mutation of (or in) a birthmark growing into a clump of malignant cells behind her right eye.

Her vision had been strange for a while. She had been very tired, too, a state she ascribed to her sadness about the loss of a new relationship.

The week before she died, Johanna showed me the notebooks this book is based on – thirteen in all – and asked me to edit and finish the text. We started transcribing the last one together, word by word, until she could no longer do it, nodding off every few seconds, her voice too weak to speak.

Thirteen grey notebooks. The last one was dated February 2022–X, a thick black X for the date she couldn't know in advance: 13 April 2022.

I brought them home and made a book from excerpts of the notebooks interspersed with my own reflections, published in Sweden in spring 2023.

The first book (2019–20) is a writer's notebook, with quotes, cuttings, reflections on style and subject, dreams, memories and meditations on the pandemic. Some passages are marked 'diary', others 'notes'. Johanna's voice feels young and experimental – there are exclamation marks and capital letters, smileys and hearts. She's happy, deeply in love with N, a translator and writer. A new relationship. Soon, however, the euphoric tone turns. N fell into a deep and uncommunicative depression, and Johanna describes her sadness and frustration. One senses the isolation of the pandemic in the background, but she has also found her subject: the notebooks now develop into a series of text fragments on the concept of loss, returning to profound feelings of bleak vulnerability, desolation and longing, intertwined with thoughts on literature and creativity.

The book is largely set during the era of Covid, and there is an unmistakable mood of the pandemic in the text – the close attention to minute details, the long meditations on the view from the window, the empty streets and the attention to soundscapes. A tree, imbued with a kind of life. Birds, observed like minor characters in a play. Dreams.

If she didn't think of the notebooks as a book from the very beginning, she soon did. From these handwritten fragments the text would later be shaped. We don't know what that book would have looked like, but it would certainly have been quite different from the one you are holding now. Her cancer diagnosis, for instance, slips in almost imperceptibly about halfway through this text. Her symptoms – a profound exhaustion and changes to her vision – had by that time been part of her life (and of the notebooks) for so long that the diagnosis feels almost like a confirmation. 'It's raining gold in my eye,' she wrote weeks before she finally saw the optician. 'All that gold, the stuff glittering in the corner of my eye. What does the fact that I saw it as beautiful rather than as a sign that there's something wrong with my vision say about me?'

Dramatic news, of course, is rarely described dramatically in diaries – those texts are a dialogue with a self that can be presumed to know the sequence of events and the dramatis personae, and the writerly attention, as in this case, may be drawn to unexpected details instead. Other times it's clear that Johanna *is* in fact writing for an audience not necessarily familiar with her family and life. She goes back and forth, and had she herself been in charge of the final text that tension, or uncertainty, would, I assume, have been ironed out. I didn't want to lose that quality of tentative searching; the sense in which the text itself reaches out in different directions – it is almost unbearably moving to me now, especially since she resolves it herself towards the end in a quiet and deeply serious acceptance of what was to come.

There are three narratives of loss in the notebooks: the loss of the presence of N as he moves from happiness, even euphoria, to a profound depression; the decline and death of Johanna's mother, and Johanna's own simultaneous arc from health to illness. Multiple nightmares run through the narrative, many of them populated with mythical creatures. Some hide their malign intent behind innocent façades (a lamb, a horse) while others are more obviously ominous

– a black dog, a sinister and lazy bear, a potentially lethal baboon mother or ambiguous owls in trees.

It is a striking feature of many of Johanna's dreams that the subject matter is often narrated rather than experienced – so, for example, she doesn't dream that she is escaping from prison, she dreams that she is *planning* an escape and then visualises, in the dream, the exact course of that imagined escape. She envisions, in two separate dreams, her daughter abandoned and alone and what the girl *would then* do. In a terrible dream about a burning body, the terror, again, is in imagining a scene she doesn't in fact see – a dream character describes, in graphic detail, what to expect from the observation of a burning body, and Johanna steels herself in anticipation. Those dreams reflect, I suppose, Johanna's profoundly narrative way of being in the world – she made her own reality (which at times could be overwhelming) real and safe by making a story out of it, as much in dreams as in waking life. But the mood of impending disaster comes back again and again, accompanied by serial attempts to work out and understand the cause of that feeling.

Margareta is a powerful presence in many of Johanna's dreams, and also in her life. Johanna's last work, *The Sentences*, is an intense and lyrical book-length essay about her mother, published in 2020. This book is in some ways a coda to that one – a more raw and immediate meditation on the vulnerability but also mysterious tenacity of her mother, the loss of language, the loss, eventually, of movement and finally almost of body.

At times, working on this book, I have imagined or thought I heard or conjured up a memory of Johanna's voice (or my own Johanna-like imitation of her voice), and sensed a dialogue between us. Then the voice would fade, leaving me with thirteen handwritten notebooks filled with dreams and fragments of text. Her notebooks are archived in the Stockholm Royal Library now. Our thousands of messages back and forth presumably still exist somewhere in the ether, digital archaeological signs, a footprint in the world. And Johanna is in me: a sensation somewhere between my heart and my throat, a mood, a word, a phrase, a hum.

A contour of my inner life.

Sigrid Rausing
London 2024

For T

=

Tanke: att avsluta terapin är att gå in
i (tillbaka? Ja, men ändå förändrad) en
gammal, nästan bortglömd värld av
känslighet, mardrömmar å ena sidan
men även en vuxenvärld av ansvar, val
vad gäller det viktiga och det mindre viktiga.
Ett ansvar för mig, T, varandet,
blivandet, gestaltandet i ett längre
perspektiv. H, försvinner JJ nu, växer
i sin frånvaro. Det är som ett träd
att luta JJ emot. Men trädet är
inte han. Det är vårt arbete. Det
vi utfört. <u>TRÄDET ÄR VÅRT ARBETE</u> !

Hon sa att JJ numera har en större
förmåga att förhålla mig på relationen
av "<u>lägre abstraktionsgrad</u>."

AND THE WALLS BECAME
THE WORLD ALL AROUND

BOOK 1: OCTOBER 2019–MARCH 2020

A thought: to finish therapy is like re-entering an old, almost forgotten world of sensitivity. A return? Yes, but it's a different place now. Nightmares on the one hand, but also an adult world of responsibility and choices, important and less important ones. T is my responsibility, her being, her becoming, her *taking shape* in a longer perspective. H, I now see, grows in his absence. Like a tree to lean against. But the tree is not him, it's our work. The thing we created together. THE TREE IS OUR WORK!

Johanna had been in psychoanalysis for a long time and was now about to finish. Her psychoanalyst, H, talks to her about trusting a 'lower degree of abstraction'.
I think of all our conversations over the years about psychoanalysis and therapy as a movement, a direction, from abstraction

to reality. What does it mean, this notion of 'being well'? To be able to live in the world as it is. To let your imagination run free rather than having to harness it to survival strategies.

This was before the pandemic, and before the illness. Johanna was already entering another world and the end of therapy was a loss, despite the image of the supporting tree, in the absence of H.

Post-analysis. Johanna lives with her daughter, who spends every other week with her father. A normal Stockholm parenting schedule.

She travels, thinks about Tel Aviv, writes in Tel Aviv. Her love for the city was partly about her father's Jewish heritage, and partly about a myth of escape and freedom, then and now:

Freedom. To be freed of the monster others perceive or project. Who are you? I answer. My answers are believed. The city, the sudden thunderstorms, the streets smelling of flowers and petrol . . .

I read and see an image: Johanna sits on a balcony in Tel Aviv or maybe Jaffa, screwing up her eyes against the sun. A glass of white wine is on the table, she is holding a notebook and a pen.

After this particular trip she sent me some additional pages for her latest manuscript, *The Sentences*, and asked for comments. I liked it and suggested she write more; said that I, as a reader, wanted to know more. The comment was part of a longer conversation between us: I wanted her writing to expand, not contract. I am thinking, again, of the direction psychoanalysis gives us, from the abstract to the concrete. Let the readers in, allow them to understand the written sense.

A little later Johanna brings her nephew to the cinema: *Maleficent 2*:

The feeling, the identification with the protagonist. The powerful love for the child. An inner loneliness, exile. A children's film. I wept. Nightmares later . . . Feathers, repulsive insects. Surrounded by beings not malevolent exactly but *blind*, blind in their instinct to protect themselves and their issue.

At times, in dreams, it's as if I clench my jaw and walk through wet concrete, slowly setting.

> Another dream. Johanna hasn't met N yet, and in this dream she is with her then boyfriend, an artist, at an art school ('colour range: white and lemon-yellow'). Another woman is interested in him and suggests that they create a joint work of art. Johanna angrily tears the plastic from a canvas and is accused of acting aggressively, while at the same time she also understands, in the dream, that she has enabled their collaboration by 'preparing' the canvas. Then I turn up in the dream, singing a duet with another student. It doesn't sound good, but that's exactly the point, she writes:

The aesthetic, the quality, was subordinate to the courage, the liveliness, the playfulness! And I felt my own stiffness, shyness, incompleteness. The unwillingness or ignorance when it comes to letting go, allowing the outer eye to close and give myself up to the moment. I felt grief and helplessness. Most of all: disappointment that I am not the person I want to be. Also: that I couldn't give S that joyful freedom!

> It is strange to read Johanna's dreams about me. No one in life gave me more of a feeling of playful freedom. And singing! We often sang. She had a strong and beautiful voice. I usually remembered the words, and she kept the tune. And it is probably true that it was mostly I who wanted to sing, to dwell in a sea of songs, memories, thoughts and feelings. Give myself up to nostalgia for the country I left so long ago.
>
> The story of this particular dream takes a graphic detour (an erotic attraction to a drag queen), then she returns to the original dream and the art school, now in the vice-chancellor's study:

. . . [He was] red-faced, portly, somewhat sweaty. A loden jacket with a round, stiff collar. He closes the door and kisses it! And I know what that means. *Thank you, faithful servant, for letting me have my way in here in secret; this room in which a special, somehow elevated and yet real, exercise of power takes place.*

The vice-chancellor paints his lips with a pale-pink lipstick: '(And isn't it precisely the shade I normally use?) Then he wants to kiss me.'

She speculates about who he is, this secretive and powerful man in lipstick. Is he more than the principle of desire, often in Swedish expressed as *begär*, a word associated with 'command', not gentle desire. The door – the faithful servant – protects the man and lets him exercise his power.

The thought of Johanna telling me this dream makes me cry again, because for all the seriousness of the underlying symbolism the sequence is absurdly funny and Johanna, at my request, would have role-played the man herself by now. Now I cry without laughing.

My dog is sleeping on the sofa. He opens his eyes when he perceives my tears and turns his head. The other dog is in the pink chair. She is sleeping, too. This story is too complicated for them, and hard to write about, because who can understand our way of seeing the dark, and laughing? Only Johanna.

Who no longer exists.

She said she would always be there.

And she was here for a while as I wrote this page, but then, like a mirage, she disappeared again.

On the next page in her notebook is another dream, about rats and puppies flowing out of a dirty hole in the floor of the bathroom at Stora Skuggan ('Great Shade'), Johanna's childhood home, a place she associated with repressed secrets, a strict aesthetic and a progressive public ethos, an atmosphere that she experienced as unsafe. The dogs – now clearly three, with 'collie-like fur' (*kolli*, in Swedish, is an old term for unaccompanied luggage, baggage, in other words, the past) – are astonishingly clean despite the dirt, but they need care. Her mother, Margareta, is there too, and Johanna shouts at her: 'You don't want to collaborate with me!'

Then she reflects again on the work, the collaboration, with H. The tree is still growing, in his absence.

And the dogs?

Stora Skuggan? Care and neglect. The lack of responsibility and of seriousness. The seriousness of love and responsibility. The long-term view. The strange thing, too, was that the puppies were so lively and clean despite the dirt and mud they had come from. They were remarkably unscathed.

A thought in my late teens: if only I had been sufficiently beautiful (a fighter pilot, a mirage), I would only have sex in public places, in the middle of a square. The sexual act instead of a monument or a fountain.

I tell a friend over a glass of wine in the kitchen, and suddenly I wonder about the words . . . To say it is also to *be* in that open square. 'To have sex', to 'relate a fantasy'. 'The fountain.'

Is exhibitionism the same thing as speaking or writing or thinking about exhibitionism? What is it to be a writer?

Amos Oz didn't want to be a writer, he wanted to be a book.

At this point – we are still in the first
notebook – N, Johanna's great new love,
enters, and the arc towards life begins to
take shape:

With an open heart, to . . . what?
See someone.
See yourself.
Feel a longing without taking shortcuts,
   to continue walking precisely in that
   direction!
To take off your clothes or take someone else's
   clothes off
open the window
describe what you see
open the fridge and in your imagination
pair ingredients, prepare them
feel love for the words . . .
the words *heart/direction/prepare*

I am in a plane. In the abdomen (yes, that's the
expression). But I think of my home as the most
exciting place of all. A container. A stage. I mean: like
seeing with your eyes shut.

And so the small world became the greatest of all worlds. The rooms are the stage for an intense drama. Here was the promised land of psychoanalysis, the world where one safely abandons oneself to another. A world where one is met in conversation, in humour and in seriousness, existential loneliness just a memory. At this moment, in these three rooms and kitchen, anything could happen. It's a fantasy of self-sufficiency. To have all your needs – the word itself felt problematic to Johanna – fulfilled. But just like Narnia's heaven (all worlds in one, forever), the fulfilled relationship lacks a certain dramatic movement. Time, hunger – the *need* – which drive the drama stop. How do you describe that?

To just once create something about love which is not about desire but rather about the sated state of fulfilled desire. But not the kind of satedness that weighs you down, like death, like sleep, like tiredness, but satisfaction as reality. A lack of fear.

S, who speaks about our normality. Normality (not convention) as defiance! The conventional makes space for obscenity. Normality, at best, is about empathy, acceptance, even time.

> Johanna's exclamation marks move me now. I let them stand. She would have let them go, I think, in the finished version, but here they are, testament to this mood, this love, this happiness.
> S is me. There are others whose names begin with S. Sofia, a close friend, is sometimes S in the book, too. But that thought about normality is mine.

The need to write, to say, to admit, to proclaim that I am in love, and then to say his name. N. To say it. To him. In him. Body and grammar simultaneously. That we will meet us/I/you/each other (at? In?)/within or in-between.

> I wish Johanna could have remained in the euphoric – the almost mystical – sense of duality for longer, but soon the atmosphere dissipates:

Unpleasant things are happening. It's like struggling against a heavy flood, my movements in the water slow, somehow paralysed, petrified. 'This is not happening,' I think, and take the entire present out [of my consciousness] leaving only literature deep inside me. But the hurt I then feel may be greater or at least as great as if I had admitted that whatever I am experiencing actually is real, and that I can both feel it *and* choose to walk away from it. To deny reality is to pave the way for something far worse in the near future.

This paragraph is undated, so I can't check it against emails or texts. But Johanna was someone who often experienced a deep sense of unease. Psychoanalysis and that arc towards normal life helped her to understand the unease, but it hadn't cured her of it.

Normal life. What does that mean, if you dream like Johanna did?

I dream about a woman in a car, with open windows and a gun in her hand. I sit on the pavement, holding a small child (T?). I am the woman's writing teacher and feel a great sense of responsibility. She lazily points the gun at me (at me *and* at the child), then she points it at herself, pushing it against her throat. I call out to her, something about the dynamic of reading and writing. About the seriousness. About value, and that it's worth it: the process, reading, the result. That whatever is said in the end has endless potential. And that, *yes*, I too know something about how painful it is to identify feelings and to come too close to something one has learnt to conceal. But whatever you hide or brush away or make less of somehow sticks to the ambivalence itself – and that stops you from becoming a great writer.

The woman presses the muzzle of the gun against her throat. It's as if she knows exactly where the carotid artery is and takes pride in that knowledge.

> Johanna has printed a few lines about psychoanalysis that I sent her and glued them to the page after this passage. 'Psychoanalysts judge the intention by the outcome, not the outcome by the intention.'
>
> Agatha Christie sometimes used the same technique. Someone is murdered, X. It looks like a mistake: the assumed victim, Y, has escaped by lucky chance. But what actually happened, Poirot (or

Miss Marple) asks. Judge the intention by the outcome. X died. Why?

2020. This is the year when I, despite (and/or because of) all the words and all the moods and all the possible ways forward will say (or try to say) the same thing every day.

Johanna wrote this before the pandemic. I wonder what she meant – what was the 'same thing' she wanted to say every day?

She has printed and glued an email exchange with H to the next page. She writes about words – *needs* and *without*. After this spare meditation on language (obliquely reminding H that *needs* are difficult for her) she carries on: 'I have to tell you that I am so very much in love. And that it's very mutual . . . It makes me . . . Well, very vulnerable and happy and entirely without a protective shell.'

She describes N. He is a writer and translator. He doesn't drink. He's very funny and yet serious and sensitive. He listens well, and he is very tender.

H writes back the same day, affirming her happiness. He ends, 'I would like to write to you about the conditions of intimacy, but strictly speaking I don't think it's necessary. I am glad that you have shifted course to the safe(r) travel routes of inner space and that you don't need to seek love in Aniara's crowded and yet so desolate halls.'

Aniara. The famous 1956 book-length poem by Swedish writer Harry Martinson, about the journey of the spaceship *Aniara* filled with evacuees from a ruined earth, irreversibly pushed off course by a collision.

An echo of the future.

Försök till räddning genom tankeflykt
och överglidningar från dröm till dröm
blev ofta vår metod.
Med ena benet dränkt i känslosvall
det andra med sitt stöd i känslodöd
vi ofta stod.

Harry Martinson,
Aniara

Attempts at respite through the flight
   of thought
and constant transference from dream
   to dream
was often our method of seeking
   relief.
With one leg steeped in a flood of
   feeling
and one supported by a lack of feeling
we often stood.

> Harry Martinson, *Aniara* (1956),
> tr. Hugh MacDiarmid and
> Elspeth Harley Schubert, 1963

Johanna's euphoria didn't last. Already on the next page she writes about her despair. How will she handle it, perhaps even (optimistic thought) value it?

How will I touch it? No one taught me care. It has to do with respect, and with time. Meanwhile, my longing steals in. And all the time I evade it . . .

I dream that I can't take care of myself . . . In the dream my outer surface breaks and people can speak about me in any way they want.

On the next page she writes about the difference between being hurt and being vulnerable.

She quotes John le Carré, who had just received the Olof Palme Prize for Achievement: 'And no one is easier to hate than a contemptible version of oneself.' He was describing Olof Palme, but also himself. Johanna recognises the feeling, and continues:

On the sofa early morning and anxiety courses through me like seawater on pebbles as the waves withdraw. I try to see it as a scene. Then the anxiety turns to grief, and it's such a relief. Grief as a restful waking dream. And then wordless calm.

(I find it difficult to write this as 'literature' since it's about something that up until now, I think, has remained unexpressed . . . talked about, but not *said*.)

My terror of imperfection in others. My terror of betrayal. My survival strategy to avoid it: stand right in it and call it something else. An anorexic strategy.

The first notebook ends with a list of twenty-two people Johanna wanted to invite for dinner to celebrate her birthday at the Academy, the Soho club. But by then England was in lockdown, and the trip was cancelled.

The Academy. We would have walked up that steep old staircase which meant something to Johanna, maybe a transition from one scene, one life, to another. You walk up the stairs and enter a room, the bar is to your left, there are tables and chairs, some old footstools. We would have been there early. I imagine the sun shining through open windows, voices from the street. We would have drunk white wine as flinty and clean as water; there would have been candles on the tables. Long before it was over, by midnight, I (always the one to suddenly long for quiet, for a book, for my own bed) would have left.

The first notebook ends with the dinner that never happened.

BOOK 2: MARCH–MAY 2020

Spring 2020. People were ill, rumours spread. There was a feeling in the air somewhere between nervousness and panic, followed by a great calm.

The days, the weeks, ran on.

Who I am *becoming* is always more important/ interesting than who I *am*. I am not sure I want to know that. Know who I am?

After that she copied a quote from David Shields's book *How Literature Saved My Life*: 'A myth is an attempt to reconcile an intolerable contradiction.'

What is it that I want to do/can do/or have to do? Above all: what is it that I don't understand? What is it that I don't take the time, or find the courage, to understand? Where is the knowledge about the past hidden?

But so much is not hidden at all. On the contrary, much is fully visible but unnamed. That's why I can walk past it (ignoring it) again and again. In that knowledge there are also statements I could protest against, or be changed by, statements that could make me more human (always this fear of inhumanity . . . that I would be lost because of it . . . or lose others).

Stoicism – the fear of vulnerability and loss of control, the wish to be cured, perhaps not so much of the fall as of the pain of the fall. (Stoicism as theatre. But also the good stoicism, the one that emerges in the face of important issues, those things we can't change.)

Without words you pass by wordless memories like statues draped in white sheets in empty rooms. You see them, and you don't see them. Johanna was afraid of what she called her inhumanity, afraid of becoming a statue draped in a sheet, a figure without emotions or vulnerability. A wordless memory. She put words to her emotions and memories in order to generate life. You might, without exaggerating, say that for Johanna writing really was about life and death.

My grandmother died at about the same age as Johanna, leaving three sons and a much-loved husband. She became a myth, my grandfather's ideal woman, beautiful, intellectual, serious. Dark-grey eyes with heavy eyelids. I think about David Shields's words: a myth is an attempt to reconcile an unbearable contradiction. A woman is loved; a woman is dead.

How do you find stoicism without performing it? How do you find authentic courage?

When Johanna fell ill, she made two decisions: to not enact courage in front of doctors she didn't know, and to not feel revulsion for the tumours. She wanted to recognise the melanoma as a part of herself, just as she wished to value (or at least respect) her own anxiety and depression. There was an element of will in this, a determination to make space for every aspect of the self. Stoicism, if you like. Or courage.

But we are getting ahead of ourselves.

None of this was in her thoughts in the spring of 2020. At that time she was thinking about her dreams, her writing and her life with a new man.

It is possible that the melanoma was already present, living its own quiet life.

Johanna adds quotes and artwork to the notebook; an article about Garry (now Garielle) Lutz, about writing becoming reality: words, sentences and passages which are not just related but which have passionate relationships with each other.

Where I would see a category mistake or some sort of linguistic synaesthesia (like hearing colours, or seeing sound), Johanna saw a new thought about creativity and passion.

On the next page is a quote from the Norwegian writer Vigdis Hjorth ('Who does not have the constant feeling that something is missing . . .'), then a cutting of Philip Guston's artwork *Legend*; a sleeping man, a horse, an empty bottle somewhat bent, perhaps a symbol for impotence and alcoholism, and patterns of holes made with nails.

Life was becoming smaller and smaller in the isolation of the pandemic. Johanna writes about the roofs on the other side of the street, about the sky and the tree that she can see from the blue chair in her living room. Something was missing, but at the same time her guilt towards her mother Margareta, who was in quarantine in a care home, had lessened:

When it's not possible to visit Mum because of the coronavirus, in other words when external circumstances force me to stay away (easing my guilt), I dream about her. And the dreams are – as ever – ambiguous, but also joyful. She speaks, we interact. She is in my life as a living human being.

Some nights ago, I dreamt about the hour of her death. Her face was turned away and there was a dark stain on her burgundy trousers. She was both old and young. Perhaps there was a sense of my childhood fear that she would die, linked to a dream of liberation – a fantasy? Death has been on his way for such a very long time – Mum's secret companion stepping up to introduce himself. Finally, they make a deal.

The dreams come and go. Johanna writes them down like reports from another country. Sometimes she reflects on them, usually not. They are almost always nightmares. Like surreal horror movies they start bright and calm but soon thicken with frightening symbolism. In one of them she is on the island of Gotland. Her mouth fills with fishy pieces of some rubbery material which turn out to be cuttlefish, *bläckfisk* or 'ink fish' in Swedish: 'And then darkness came, very quickly, the moon hidden by light clouds. I spat out the cuttlefish, all the little white pieces, on a large and unfamiliar courtyard paved with cobblestones.'

I think of the cuttlefish as writing, the pieces the short stories she was working on. But Johanna wakes up and thinks about N and her feelings of abandonment and sadness. The fracture in the foundation. Spitting out food. 'Always that image, both metaphorically and in real life,' she writes. 'Shame around needs, around exposure.'

Nothing much happens in her life, or

in anyone's life for that matter. A drunk neighbour calls her *dear heart*, says her hair looks nice, spills beer and fumbles at the wrong door.

Was that the arc towards normal life we had talked about?

She dreams about her mother again. Margareta is on a hospital bed in a temporary ward at the airport, with many other patients. She sees Johanna through a window and smiles, a surprised and happy smile. Johanna signals a heart with her hands and then wonders about the sign – was it too youthful, a TikTok gesture? But it doesn't matter: 'In the dream I loved her, and it was simple and obvious, and it was good to feel love.'

Dreams, dreams. She is on a passenger boat in the archipelago on a canal between islands, a frozen landscape. 'At times we come out to the open sea, I can see the silhouette of Stockholm on the horizon.' You can hear music, sad music, and Johanna can't defend herself against it:

Is it more difficult for me than for the others? It's as though the message of the music is that there is no point in living but that it will protect me, or at least be present when I die. It's as though the music is calling forth a dying, composing a possible suicide without quite expressing it (because it's only notes, no words). My eye is drawn to the surface of the water, the grey expanse. I can't see details. It's as though I am falling or sinking, as if some middle layer has been dissolved. Next to me is a director. Suddenly she sees what is happening with me (she's conscious of it, but immune!). She resolutely stands up, pushes through rows of passengers and asks the captain to turn the music off. And as soon as the music stops, everything changes.

In the next dream Johanna is with friends, talking about books – three books – when she suddenly becomes overwhelmed with tiredness. In the dream she falls asleep and then dreams that she wakes up, which gives the scenario a curious feeling of reality:

I didn't resist the tiredness, I let it come and wash over me. The next morning, I woke up. I had forgotten T.

I couldn't help that I had fallen asleep, but I had still committed a crime and was guilty of a betrayal. The feeling of free fall . . . I called her, and her voice sounded empty, disillusioned, monotonous. She had looked for me everywhere, she said, and then she had fallen asleep on the bed and gone to school the next morning. I said, 'I'm so sorry! Forgive me! I have nothing to say in my own defence. There's nothing I can do. I wasn't drunk, I didn't forget you, I was just so tired. Well, I did forget you in my sleep. But I couldn't help falling asleep. We have to see a psychologist! We need help!'

I knew I introduced the idea of a psychologist in the monologue because I couldn't bear the hurt I had caused her, couldn't bear to be in the pain, the impossible pain. The loss. That sense of something unfinished and broken. My guilt.

I walked along the sea on a beach of gravel and shells and saw Stockholm on the horizon. There she was, but it was as if I would never get hold of her. Never reach her.

The analysing object, the tree Johanna was leaning against, is growing in the absence of analysis. She thinks about what it means not to be able to undo loss. She thinks about her dream, the friends, the wine, the books, the wide grey sea. 'The responsibility and the guilt about losing the most important thing when I close my eyes.'

On the next page she adds: 'When I fell asleep, i.e. became human, I became inhuman.'

What actually is a guilt complex? I don't remember conversations with Johanna about guilt. The idea of it had become a worn-out joke, a cultural platitude. We experienced guilt without (together) naming it, without speaking and thinking about what it meant and where it came from.

Guilt about absence. To involuntarily fall asleep, drifting away from responsibility. An echo of the future.

In the next dream T has had an offer from the Italian secret police to entrap drug dealers who will later be questioned under torture. T has to be present during the interrogations. At first it's exciting, T acts her role, but then slowly the scene becomes unbearable. Johanna tries to pull her away and is accused of being hysterical. She feels – again – a great tiredness:

. . . as though I was about to fall asleep. A heavy feeling, as though my face was covered in clay. And I know that the weight is connected to sadness but also to holding on to my own reality.

I run through a town, all cities in one. I can't find my way; can't remember the name of the area where we live. There are big signs everywhere and maps, but they only show the local streets with churches and places of interest. Was the name of our street something to do with *old*, or with *Jewish*? I don't know the name in Italian. I take a random underground train and come to a modern shopping centre. I run, searching – there is the sea! On a side street I find one of the plain-clothes policemen. He puts a finger over his lips to indicate that I must be quiet. He has a black eye. Some young people drive past me in a car, shouting, 'You have some free time! Go to the cinema! The next film starts in a minute – you have enough time, if you can find it . . . ha, ha, ha! One o'clock. Matinee. A children's film.'

There is her tiredness again, and the guilt. Does she somehow sense her illness? I don't know. This type of melanoma can grow fast or slowly, and it can be near-dormant for a long time. I know that Johanna, to help her tiredness and back pain, started to train more, lifting weights until she could lift the equivalent of her own weight at the gym.

I couldn't follow her into that world, and she could barely make it herself, even in her dreams:

I dreamt about writing and training. I was at the gym, and so desperately tired. But I also know other writers, all women, who cycle for miles through the dark and the rain. The staff at the gym are all proofreaders and editors doubling up as personal trainers, Olympic swimmers and professional dancers. I am so terribly tired, I just want to sleep, can't keep awake.

That modest view . . . the angular field, the image of the garden at Stjärnan. The apples on the tree were transparent, you could see right through to the core. I imagined them lit up at night. Apple stars with cores made of stars.

The crossroad, the field, the woods, the coolness of the earth cellar . . . it was as if it oozed coolness.

Stjärnan (the Star) was Johanna's grandparents' home, where she had lived as a small child. The original home.

More dreams:

A woman humiliates her.

Jakob, Johanna's brother, is ill.

A plane makes an emergency landing:

I see meadows, oaks, sheep. I see grass, then individual blades of grass. A few are yellow in a sea of green. Then I understand. And I am not frightened, not for one moment. We run through a fence, we run down gravestones in a churchyard, we cross an empty parking lot in an abandoned shopping centre.

Then she has a nightmare about me. I have a big workroom, which reminds her of her mother's room. I am working and want to be left in peace, pointing silently at the door. Johanna leaves but then she comes back again, thinking that *she* will not disturb me. Others might, but she will not. She is the exception. She steals into my bathroom, takes some of my Clinique cream. But I am angry when I see her and expel her with a hoarse voice, shouting *out, out, out, out, out!*

My room, my work, my asylum, my clinic. And I too turn inhuman with my corvid cries.

In another dream she is driving with her mother:

A muddy wide road descending towards a small bridge and dark water. The car glides on to the bridge which gives way, overturning the car into the water. Mum is next to me, seatbelt on. I have the thought that I am killing her. My grandmother is in the car next to us, a grey blue little Golf. We were driving at the same speed, but she was able to stop. She made it. Then it occurs to me that she is already dead.

Book 2 ends with a response from the eminent psychiatrist and author Johan Cullberg. They have met, but it's not clear why Johanna wrote to him. She may have just read his interesting memoir about his mentally ill brother. She seems to have mentioned in her letter that she felt that she had 'dead stains' inside her and Cullberg does his best to reassure her that no one does: 'I understand that you are writing metaphorically, but sometimes metaphors can take on their own life,' he writes. 'No living person has any dead parts. But of course, one may try to kill the memories, or whatever the memories represent.'

Johanna's *stains* have become the neutral 'parts' in his response. There is something very sympathetic about that small movement from 'stains' to 'parts'.

Johanna probably already had a stain, a lesion, behind her right eye.

You are *dead* for such a short while, maybe ten or fifteen years at most. Then you become one of those who passed away and disappeared a long time ago, except for your child, who will always say their mum died.

Maybe it's a way for the child to prolong the mother's existence. Not life, but some kind of identity or being.

What was it Rilke wrote about the strange nature of *being dead*?

It is truly strange to no longer inhabit
    the earth,
to no longer practise customs barely
    acquired,
not to give a meaning of human
    futurity
to roses, and other expressly
    promising things:
no longer to be what one was in
    endlessly anxious hands,
and to set aside even one's own
proper name like a broken plaything.
Strange: not to go on wishing one's
    wishes. Strange
to see all that was once in place,
    floating
so loosely in space. And it's hard
    being dead,
and full of retrieval, before one
    gradually feels
a little eternity. Though the living
all make the error of drawing too
    sharp a distinction.
Angels (they say) would often not
    know whether

they moved among living or dead. The
    eternal current
sweeps all the ages, within it, through
    both the spheres,
forever, and resounds above them in
    both.

Rainer Maria Rilke, *Duino Elegies* (1911–22),
            the first elegy, tr. A. S. Kline, 2001,
                    Poetry in Translation

BOOK 3: MAY–AUGUST 2020

Now: a fly crawls over my foot and onto my wrist and I can't feel it. I see it but I can't feel it and it makes me feel like I'm a tree. Another kind of being.

What happens now?

All the notes on my phone: what's the story? Could one draw any conclusions from them? Sense anything? Make a diagnosis?

The revelation of private notes: the ego rolls over on its back showing its underbelly.

> Like an insect, she writes. Or like Totoro.
>
> Then she makes notes for a short story about the horror of the dentist's drill:

But the fear flickering past is not the condition . . . Saliva sucked out, terror like sand in the mouth. Ash covers the thought or was it the heart. Something disastrous is happening to her. Desolating, empty, emptier than empty.

I remember a conversation with Johanna about her sudden fear of the dentist, the drill, the thought that the tooth *was a stone*. I remember and hesitate about the memory but something, after all, is being said here. Presentiments of death are everywhere in these notebooks.

When Johanna was dying, she stopped dreaming. I asked her what happened in her nights without dreams. Just blackness, she said. Black as night.

But what was her dying but a terrifying nightmare of tumours hard as stones under the skin, under the membrane of the liver; satellites from the eye (seeing, consciousness).

The next passage begins as prose, then turns into a poem:

Useless memories.
Citrus fruit embedded in ice or thrown
    against someone's window
late one night in the hope of – what?
Composting with confidence. Organic
    breakdown is slow this far north.
I go back and rest my hand on the inside of
    the orange peel
cool as a sheet
glistening listening white.

No one can speak about
That acid moving
Through the body some
Mornings
In every act – a corrosive substance
An image in a pane of glass: is that me?
    My friend? The mother of my friend?
Is it the acids from the dream
See your child disappear on a
Road in a park at night
Chestnut trees in flower and the dark
Stretch out in deranged
Longing for unity accordance
The circle of trees
They are not I they are not

Me
Standing in the dream by the subway
    entrance falling
Towards a wordless mistake.
Here: no one has ever been able to
Speak about that acid
Thinning before it dissolves
The involuntary interior flight.
Forget about the self then come back to it.
Wake the child. Drink coffee.
In the dream it's always night.
Look someone in the eye and watch
    something fracture. And heal during
    the day.

And heal during the day. There is Johanna's
resolute inner director again. The death-
affirming hypnotic music is turned off;
there is hope.
There *will* be hope.

Now she is in my summer house by the
sea, without me. The pandemic makes
travel difficult, but Johanna is here with
N, happy. Euphoric, even.

The kite! To be free enough to say: we will not leave until we've seen the kite. And then we wait, for days or for months. The kite decides.

Oh kite, I am so happy!

I think of myself as an animal to get away from gender, but surely animal life is all about gender. Roles? No, genetically imprinted behaviour. One would probably be killed for not following instinct. In the human kingdom the opposite is true.

Stoicism . . . to wish for *everything* but pretend that nothing matters.

I dream about a little girl (like me in that photo with Mum in *Vi Läser*, helmet haircut, big eyes, red cheeks). A child with 'powers' whose name is Onda [evil]. It's pronounced Ånda.

The place: a conference hotel. I carry the child even though she can walk, conscious of the pleasure of her weight in my arms. After a while I start to worry about her parents missing her. We walk through the rooms looking for them. I don't know what they look like. I ask the girl to help, making it a game so that she will not – even for a moment – feel lost. Information: the mother has long, dark hair. The father is a lawyer and one of the important people at the conference.

He is regarded as strict. A judicial drama is going on between a composer and a conductor, something about intellectual property rights and sexual harassment. The writers (because it's also a writers' conference, maybe something to do with PEN) are all agreed that one of them (the composer?) is innocent. I don't understand how they can be so certain. Why is everyone of the same view? How can it be so simple?

We find the child's mother, who waves and smiles but makes no other sign that she wants to take Onda. We find the father in an office. Then I lose the child in the zone between the parents. The zone, which is the whole hotel. I look for her. The zone of unclear responsibility. *Area of responsibility.*

I tell the dad that I am the only person there who is really not sure about who the guilty party is, the composer or the conductor. He's a criminal defence lawyer and says he's confident the case is the opposite to what everyone else believes. But he's open to the possibility that he is wrong. He says I should look for Onda on the second floor. He comes with me but shows no sign that he is going to help me search. He touches my shoulder in the lift. Then he looks at me and somehow caresses my contours in the air. It's so extraordinarily inconsistent and somehow compulsive, the fact that he, an analytical and honest lawyer (a human rights activist!) is also a man who is hot for me in a lift when we (I!) are looking for a (his!) lost child.

(The small child Onda . . . the evil child. The child who aches . . . I.)

> Evil doll was a phrase we played with. Evil doll, from *Child's Play*. *Evil doll*, Johanna would say. I am not sure I always knew what she meant, but it was funny anyway. An innocent face masking mock-evil intent. But now I am thinking about the child Onda, pronounced Ånda, and the words *vånda* and *ångest*, *ånger* and *andas* come to mind. Agony, anguish, regret and breathing.
>
> I am also thinking of the dream about the death-affirming music, the composition generating a possible (unexpressed) suicide. At that point, the resolute inner director stepped in and turned the music off. This dream contains a judicial drama about intellectual property rights and sexual harassment, a case between a composer and a conductor. The composer is generally thought to be in the right, the

conductor in the wrong; Johanna is not sure. We don't know their gender.

Intellectual property rights: *upphovsrätt* in Swedish. Good word, one of us would have said, had we discussed this dream. A word that defines the right to creative work, but which also hints at childhood via the association with origins (*upphov*), but also with needs (*behov*).

I think about Johanna's parents, and the divorce. The idea of right and wrong in the dream, the idea of a crime. The story of a composer and a conductor behind the story of the parents who seem to have so very little interest in the lost Onda. Children's right to get their needs recognised. The right to have needs.

This summer: nothing more to wish for. Miracle days.

A dream: a shallow grey sea, flotsam, things or parts of things. Is this the image corresponding to the words *fragments of memory*? It looks . . . unusable. No clues, just stuff that's in the way.

Parts of things. I think about Johan Cullberg's rewording of Johanna's 'dead stains' as 'parts'. Parts of oneself.

Johanna is holding a beautiful old stone handle in her dream, it's heavy and smooth in her hand. Someone has written a magazine piece about her:

The language is careless, almost incomprehensible. N offers to edit it – a relief – but almost nothing in the text has anything to do with me. It's a sort of lifestyle piece, dizzy, vertiginous even, while everything I want to write about, everything I want to say, has to do with this stone handle, so cool to the touch, so safe, yet also somehow so incomprehensible.

Why do I start crying at this point in the notebook? I think about my own nightmare some nights ago, which Johanna would have helped me to understand. My loneliness without her. 'Talk?' one of us would text. 'Yes!' the other would answer, '5 min,' she might add. 'Just making coffee!' Then we'd begin. The dreams, the books, the people, the writing. And now she is gone.

Then she was still in my house, the house we still sometimes call Sten's house after the architect who built it and lived there every summer until he died. *Sten* means stone. The stone handle. A firm grip.

The landscape, she writes. The affection. To absorb it all. The people. Johanna felt euphoric in that timeless coastal landscape of Bronze Age graves, stone and rocks, juniper and closely cropped grass. The cattle move back and forth on the common, walkers pass by, seagulls cry. Every year is the same year.

But then she dreams that she and N 'destroy' my house. I am there, and again, unforgiving:

She is trying to find a place where she can be undisturbed. There is none. Someone has walked around in trainers and there are traces of mud everywhere. And the assurance that it will be all right, that it's just a matter of cleaning it up, is absent.

Johanna walks by the sea in her dream, weighed down by responsibility and a form of guilt, she writes, that seems especially designed for her. 'I have to take responsibility even for that'.

Do I have to take responsibility for her dreams about me?

Later she dreams that she is on a boat and that there are dangerous swirls of current on the dark water. T's little dog has come back from the dead. She's like one of Rilke's angels, not knowing whether she is walking amongst the living or the dead:

She is not quite alive. Some sense of presence is lacking. It's as if our memories and ties to her have been erased. Anaesthesia of the soul and of the skin.

Then she dreams about a young woman, who might be the writer Fleur Jaeggy:

She's in her late teens or maybe twenty and she is rehearsing a role. She is supposed to move in a dance. She is being filmed. Behind her is a long band of ribbon, a film trick even though it's theatre. She doesn't pull the ribbon, it follows her, snakes around her, seeks her out. A snake. A lead. She speaks to it, insipid words in a childish voice. I know her a bit, and I also have a small role in the film as a border policewoman. I'm supposed to ask for her passport, look at her face, and then, with a gesture, let her in. Her acting is also an entrance examination of some kind (perhaps to an acting school). I tell her that speaking doesn't really work, it just gets in the way. It doesn't tell us anything. Could she make sounds instead? The ribbon snakes after her, forms a ring round her, she runs away from it, she ignores it, she hums and moans, makes faint animal sounds.

We were both reading Fleur Jaeggy that summer. Johanna quotes from the novel *Proleterka*: 'Nothingness is not empty. As if fallen from the talons of a bird of prey in flight, thoughts drop into our mind when we are convinced that we are not thinking.'

She returns to Stockholm, visits Margareta at her care home and describes what she sees there:

A dead person is carried out on a stretcher, covered with a dark-brown cloth. I instinctively felt that it was wrong to cover the face with cloth. Death had already occurred. It was no longer a private battle. There was no breathing. Why can't the face be amongst us?

On the street cars without permits were being removed. Objects and human beings . . .

> I think of the Swedish word *människa*, more evocative than 'person' and less emphatic than 'a human being'. I consider substituting 'corpse', or simply 'body' for 'a dead person' in the sentence above, but what Johanna was getting at is exactly that in-between state in Rilke's poem, the continued humanity of 'the dead'.
>
> *I may be dead but I'm still me*, she might have said (as a dead person) at the hospice. She was lying there, smiling ironically, as the rest of us hugged, bewildered, telling each other the story of her dying.
>
> Who said that catastrophe is endless narration?

Darkness. Images. Clumps (clusters) of objects, faces. What will I think about, to what will I return in my memory when I am old? Or: what images will seek me out, linger, ask to be seen?

There it is again, memories as 'clumps', an ugly word. Flotsam. In the way. But what is she getting at?

After this, a dialogue:

'You are not afraid of dark water.'

'No, but I want to *understand* dark water. And it's the effort of trying to understand which frightens me. I am afraid that I won't have the strength to understand. I'm afraid that I won't have the strength to live with the understanding.'

Those were the kind of sentences that could make me say calming things to Johanna. Come back from abstractions and think instead about your capacity to describe.

Sometimes I tried, maternally or ironically, to pull her back to life, to concrete matters. Now I feel afraid, too – afraid of not having the strength to understand Johanna's writing, her dreams, her state of mind, her intentions. The dreams slide between us. Last night I dreamt her dream of a small child slipping out of my hands; felt the joy of holding it (a warm and steady weight), then the terror of forgetting it or dropping it, a body slipping, falling.

The notebooks are frightening, an archive of the dark matter she pulled into the light, forcing herself to see. She made herself think and write about it, she wanted to be strong and resolute, to have the emotional strength to read reports about war and atrocities, but she could barely do it. Her visual imagination was too strong; she saw too much.

My son Daniel called her *my Hanna* when he was little. He thought Johanna (the Swedish J is soft) meant 'your Hanna'; his Hanna who gave his plastic dinosaurs funny voices, who cooked and sang and made the whole house warmer and livelier. Where is she, our Hanna, in these despairing text fragments?

Most of them are undated, but on August 4th, a year and a month before the diagnosis, she wrote about death. She is still in our house by the sea:

Some days I forget that I am going to die. Like just now, when I thought about the house, and the landscape outside. The sea, the common. The horizon. I will always be there. Or at least for an unimaginably long time – a vast stretch of time disappearing into light. I and the landscape will remain. It is such a strange feeling to both imagine that and to believe it, at least for a while.

The next night, a terrible nightmare:

A body is going to be burnt on a plastic mattress. The room is some kind of business premise, a shop, emptied out. A florist? There are some pots with basil in a corner. I worry about the smoke, the flesh, the plastic. I also wonder why we are here. Why do we have to witness this? Because it's good to learn how to handle it. To watch the details of a body burning is honing and some kind of test of my maturity, my openness, my robust attitude to death.

But why do the children have to be here, in the smoke? Is the door to the yard unlocked? We have to be able to get out. The door to the street will be blocked with people.

Yes, the door to the yard is open.

Someone tells us what we are about to see. The skin

wrinkling, bubbling, fat boiling, the sound of sinews snapping. What will happen with the lips, the eyes, the hair, and liquids that will dry up or come out.

> The last line peters out and Johanna crossed it out: 'I wonder if it will help me to somehow intrude with my eyes, or'
>
> She doesn't actually witness the fire in the dream, but she is forced to listen to the narrative of what will happen with the dead body as it burns. The story peters out when she wonders if it will *help* to keep watching, to not look away from the terrible events. There is potency in courage.
>
> I think about the pots of basil, *basilika* in Swedish. At one time Roman basilicas were law courts. Later they were used for other things, but *basilika* feels like a clue to justice, maybe to human rights, the pot (*kruka*), Swedish slang for cowards. Johanna was aware of the courage needed for testimony. But did she have the strength to do it? The words made a forced entry into her mind, creating images no one should be made to see.

She is still in our house by the sea with N, and T is there too. Now, a miracle:

We swam in phosphorescence. It was like fireworks on a film played backwards; it's there, like glowing little lamps, and you don't see where it comes from. Suddenly it's there, and then it's not! It's so beautiful, so new, that you just laugh.

She sent me a picture of T dancing in a white sheet. It's the end of summer. 'The cool of the night lingers under the bramble in the mornings,' she wrote, and told me about the neighbours, the farmers' cattle, the luminescence in the sea and how much she loves the cracked old steps leading up to the house from the common.

All the words, all the specific words we looked for and found (discovered), all the words we uttered and put to one side: we said them, and when they were said (after being found) it was as if they had always been there (like any old thing) and we forgot that at one time or other we had found them – that there was a time before we found them.

The stamp pad when I was little. A flat white tin box. The damp captured, resting and prepared, in the closed box.

Death is that stamp. The ink bleeds, stains. The death of our dog. The thought of my mother's death. The stamp.

A memory. A *part* of a memory, a non-speaking memory.

BOOK 4: AUGUST–DECEMBER 2020

The fourth notebook begins with a quote from the poet Robert Hass, in the *Paris Review*: 'It takes will, sometimes, to put yourself in the place where poetry might happen.' I listen to his voice – a Poetry Foundation recording of the long poem 'Faint Music'. The voice and the poem are extraordinarily beautiful, each reflecting the other. With whom can I speak about this particular combination of sound and text, in Johanna's absence? A hundred people, and not one who would instantly understand my reaction to it.

Maybe you need to write a poem
    about grace.

When everything broken is broken,
and everything dead is dead,
[...]
I had the idea that the world's so full
     of pain
it must sometimes make a kind of
     singing.
And that the sequence helps, as much
     as order helps—
First an ego, and then pain, and then
     the singing.

> Robert Hass, 'Faint Music',
> from *Sun Under Wood* (1996)

Johanna has glued a 1930s photograph of a Jewish soldier from Kurdistan to the next page. His scarf is woven, a pattern of two repeated symbols: a circle with a dot in the middle (a representation of the I from Kabbalah) and a white dot, the creation. The I and the beginning.
She thinks of the dot as a white pupil.

Memories. *Not* nostalgia. The opposite. Fear of memories. They have to be dredged up and put in a drawer, in the right place. The au pair who gave us liquorice lollipops at Skansen. My brother's face, sticky and black. The lollipop glistening mother-of-pearl, black and grey. An image of destruction. How she misunderstood and distorted us. Her seeming innocence, her sly manoeuvres. We became the children of others, not just other people's children.

The boats on the quay (Söder Mälarstrand) cry in their moorings. (The seagulls sound like children too.)

Someone calls from Karolinska hospital to say that a parent has died. I don't know if it's my father or my mother.

It's my mother. She's in a barracks outside the main building. There is a folder on her chest: 'Patient of the female gender. In a coma.'

So, she's alive? She is curled up as though afraid, dark circles under her eyes. I hold her hand, put my cheek against hers. I say, 'Mum, do you remember the flowers? The spring flowers, *Scilla siberica*, yellow star-of-Bethlehem, and the one that was blue, a light light blue like white laundry coloured blue in the wash. Like scilla?'

Then she opens her eyes, smiles with them. Staff enter, frightening, dirty people with malicious eyes, long, greasy hair, dirty fingernails. And she is so frightened of them, curling up like a small child. I don't know what to do. I don't know what I *can* do. But I do know that if I could only be alone with her, I could keep her alive.

> Johanna uses the expression *sorgkantade*, 'edged with grief', for dirty fingernails. Good word: see how effectively she brings grief into the dream, hiding it behind coma and fear and scilla and yellow star-of-Bethlehem and that nameless flower, light light blue like white laundry coloured in the wash.
>
> Like forget-me-not.

A dream:

The most idyllic but also mysterious cottage you could imagine. It's built of dark timber on rocks high up in the mountains. There is an open fire and white curtains over the windows, much worn but carefully ironed. Someone says, 'We are old now, sometimes we get help with the cleaning. They enjoy coming up here, you know. The house is empty.'

I need the loo. There is an earth closet outside. The outhouses are linked with metal poles straddling crevices. It's pitch-black outside. The round, bare rocks glimmer faintly in the light from the fireplace, but a few steps away from the house there is total darkness. There is something treacherous about the softness of the rocks, as treacherous as a sea, soft, hilly waves that can drown you. Here you can slide down, die in a crevice, fall headlong down a precipice. But there are no sharp angles. Everything is soft and rounded. Like a shoulder, a knee, a skull.

Dawn, or at least some light. I will pee outside. But when I turn round, I can't see where I came from. There is no path, only these rounded stone formations everywhere. If I take a wrong turn I may be lost forever.

I am not falling but I am swaying from side to side and back and forth. Things fall apart. My eyes are not unsteady, it is some fracture in reality itself. It comes and goes. Nothing holds me, not even my own surface tension. I don't feel anything breaking, trickling, but I am somehow diluted. Something shimmers, evaporates.

Shimmers.

> Is this a dream, or a waking state of mind? I don't know. But those of us who sometimes find ourselves in fragile or desolate states of mind are given to believing that what we feel in our bodies

is a reflection or an effect of what we feel in our inner selves: we suspect a psychosomatic episode or condition. But there are clues to the contrary here and there in Johanna's notebooks. *My eyes are not unsteady, it is some fracture in reality itself.* Something real is happening in her body. Something *shimmers*, already now.

To predict somebody's absence. The exercise in grief, the training in loss. T, who leant against the curtain and the window behind. What if it had been open, I think. The window. What if the window had been open.

A note, dated September 2nd, is recorded after a 'hellish nightmare':

The world remains unreal unless I call it into being. To not be met in conversation creates an avalanche of grief, panic and destructiveness. But why don't I stop the process? I close myself off and cry floods of internal tears. A child abandoned and ignored. Disregarded. Why don't I say that it hurts? Because the darkness would then be exposed to light? A leakage? A taste for blood amongst us?

This is also part of me. I always forget. My Achilles' heel. (Competent and wounded. I'd like to be less competent, and for the wound to be more visible.)

> What has happened? Johanna was at the Jewish Centre to listen to an author, and she had been recording her last book as an audiobook. N had rented a small flat in her neighbourhood. 'N woke me from a nightmare last night,' she wrote to me. 'But I loved recording the book. Some parts I had almost forgotten. Talk soon!! Xxx'
> She sent a picture of the view from the recording studio. I don't think about the nightmare, don't ask her about it, just comment, absently, on the photo: 'Amazing sky! Xxx'
> *Amazing sky.* She tried to tell me, but there was so much I didn't hear.

Years of dreams, nightmares about desolation and perhaps injustice. To be an outcast or to be forced into exile, leaving everything behind.

I am wounded, carried by soldiers on a stretcher through towns and villages. Someone walks beside me and touches my nipples. They turn hard as stones.

A black dot which suddenly lights up. Will it detonate, explode? To run without making a sound, holding your breath.

I think about the 1930s picture of the Jewish soldier in Kurdistan. The shining pupil, the white dot, creation itself.

September 2020. It's a year before the diagnosis. Johanna is misreading words and wonders why, reflecting on the psychoanalytic significance of what she sees or doesn't see. She notices other strange signs or symptoms:
She blows out a candle that was not burning.
She mistakes a loo roll for a glass.
She drops a sharp knife which punctures a floorboard and stands vibrating between her feet.

I dreamt about a lamb in a flock of lambs. It sought me out and bit my arm. It hurt so much. A human bite, dangerous. I had to grip the lamb's nose, try to hurt it to make it let go.

> According to psychoanalytic object relations theory, warm and stable early relationships create inner 'good objects', a safe interior atmosphere. Experiences of abandonment or violence create 'bad objects': enduring, at times permanent, feelings of desolation and anxiety. The 'bad objects' can be represented in dreams as malicious beings, often masked as innocent and good.
> Like the lamb.
> Like the dark, round cliffs, treacherously dangerous.
> Evil doll horror film scenarios: malevolence hidden behind an innocent façade.

I don't want to be a woman and not sure I want to be human. I take the laundry out of the washing machine, put a pillowcase on the radiator, tuck it in. A caring, tender gesture. Against my will. I am . . . or . . . I would like to be.

Or not to have to be at all.

A crisis. The thought: if I were an animal, I would be inedible. Saturated with adrenaline, anguish, anxiety. A bitter, inedible animal.

> Mid-October 2020. Johanna stays in my house by the sea again, and her mood slowly lifts. Her dreams are calmer, but an undertone of desolation remains:

Dream: A school. Some literate children had scrawled admonishments and slogans for their parents in the hall. None of them, it seemed, were able to look after their children.

'The Talmud says, dreams which are not interpreted are like letters which have not been opened.' Erich Fromm. To investigate something in a text is not the same thing as posing a question and answering it. You might expose something (a problem, a scene, an emotion), and then allow the text to do its work, without further analysis.

December 1st, 2020. I dreamt that I fell into water, that I allowed myself to fall. From a jetty, in bright sunshine. Some people are standing on the jetty. (Relatives, not my parents. Or is the man over there my father? He slides into the image of relatives, belongs to the group, but is not distinguishable as someone who has a particular tie to me.) There are no ties.

I sink below the surface. I see corals, mussels, stones, seaweed. The water is so clear. I can reach the bottom but I let myself float on my back, half lying down. I see the jetty and the people through the water, flickering, swaying bodies. I climb up the steps. My mother is there. A man, my boyfriend. They hold on to me, carefully, lovingly. They are sitting and I lie down between them.

My mother. My boyfriend. Two kinds of love.

Then I fall into the water, I let myself fall. I swim underwater. It's so clear. When I stand up, I see the people on the jetty. Strangers I am related to. 'It's important not to let it stick,' a woman says, and I understand what she means. What mustn't stick is the habit of falling, the habit of disappearing under the surface. To gain attention? To be singled out, to show off? My need for love. 'Don't let it stick.' That is to say, don't let them become a habit, these needs, these desires, these wishes, these falls.

Perhaps we can analyse the dream – the fall into the water, the flickering, swaying

77

bodies on the jetty – differently. A premonition. Not a supernatural sign but a form of awareness, situated somewhere between body and thought. Not static knowledge but a signal, a faint Morse code picked up by the unconscious and reproduced and mixed up in a dream.

It's nine months before the diagnosis.

BOOK 5: DECEMBER 2020–JANUARY 2021

I am crawling through passages on top of a bazaar. Ventilation pipes, attic corridors, negative shapes. What is convex here is a valve or a cupola in the space below me. The surface is glossy and slippery, and I have to concentrate. I make my way up some rounded steps; press the flats of my hands against the walls to keep my balance. I hear the sound of running water from somewhere. The light is indirect, and there are no shadows. I am moving through the 'lining', the wrong side of the body of a house. But it is also a brain. I'm in the space between the skull and the brain. Outside someone else's thoughts? Have I missed the entrance? Is the brain N's? I feel my desperate, illegitimate wish to be allowed in.

Days of feeling raw and naked, yes. Days of uncertainty, the fear of being abandoned. The fear that our light will be extinguished.

December 15th, 2020. Orpheus and Eurydice. I am Orpheus. N is in the underworld. If I look at him, he will disappear. Is that the image of togetherness in a depression? That the person weighed down by depression can't bear to be heard or seen with love? It's as though the shell has to remain intact, otherwise the self will cease to be.

December 18th, 2020. Slept, and woke up again. Thought: now I have to rein in my heart. I will frost it, until it's unflinching and several degrees cooler.

The dizziness is like a wind from the unconscious.

I feel like a ship with engine failure still quietly gliding forwards in the right direction. But now there are rocks under the water. They were not there before, or were they? I have to force myself to admit that I don't know. Were they there?

I write (but only to myself): it's hard to long for someone if you don't know whether they are coming back. The longing turns into grief. And the grief, I suppose, is a process of healing. When I am done with grieving, whatever it was that I wanted to come back to might not exist any more.

I have come to understand my mind's way of managing life: after a few hours of sad and helpless thoughts some defensive thoughts emerge. Then, happy thoughts: It is what it is. It will be fine. It will be fine.

> 'It is what it is.' Johanna's friend K began her speech at the memorial with those words. Johanna had told her about the terminal prognosis, K had screamed, and Johanna had said, very calmly, *It is what it is.*
>
> What does that degree of stoic courage and resilience mean?

Here's a difficult thing: to know what level of grief and longing and betrayal I am experiencing. Betrayal. It's the first time I've had the courage to use that word. The first time I believe in its importance. To betray, yes. But to be betrayed!

If you come back, I will just be happy. I will say, 'How you frightened me!'

When he comes back all this will frighten him. Because surely the loss of a loving relationship must be frightening once you can access your feelings? To have so nearly lost me.

What am I to him now? A dark house. All the lights turned off. But still some sort of body.

My vanity: that I would be his home. My strength: that we would be each other's home. Not in an ostentatious or tense way, but just as a given. Something *given*.

I fantasise about sending a question: will you love me (again)? And that the answer will be: Yes.

The dream about the baby. I love it and look after it, but it breaks, hits its face against a stone. Blood and mud on its face. The mouth is full of blood. The baby speaks, says: 'I am bleeding between the legs, too.'

I don't know if it's a girl or a boy, but the baby is broken inside.

The risk of thinking so much about another person is that you suddenly know (or think you know) more about them than they know themselves. That might not be true. Or even if it is, your thoughts might be too neat. Schematic insights that should have been allowed to emerge in some other way.

A lack of care. That I should be so careless.

The danger Johanna reflected on in relation to N is the same danger I have thought about in relation to her notebooks. I, too, am worried about drawing the wrong conclusions and that I am writing too much instead of letting the notebooks speak for themselves. That it's all too tidy, or that I lack care.

'But listen,' Johanna would have said. 'We are writing this together! Just play with it . . .'

Johanna came from a family where any experience was seen as potential writing material whereas I come from a family where silence and discretion were and are more highly valued. But when N was unresponsive and Johanna wrote messages into a void, she thought about the questions I have had to reflect on in my writing life. 'To claim the right to speak,' she wrote.

To be someone who does the wrong thing. To do something that feels right but which turns out to be wrong. Like saying that I miss you when you can't receive my longing. It's as though I distracted you in the middle of a tricky balancing act. It's like trying to restore contact with an astronaut lost in space. The shorter and more precise the message is, the greater the chance that it will reach its destination, and the less the risk that it will be misunderstood.

The danger: my greed. I must remember Orpheus and Eurydice. Not to turn round and look. I think: what will I see?

> *What will I see.* Not what *would* I see if I turned round (which I am not allowed to do), but what *will* I see. Better to see your lover disappear than to see nothing at all. There's the clarity of vision, and the obligation to narrate, to describe.

To know who you are and to have a broken heart. Readiness is not about defence, it's about observation. To be fifty and strong, protecting joy and protecting grief.

To rest in the air currents, at peace in the absence of thoughts. To rest, arms straight, on the bench press.

I could divide and subdivide each event and statement, each confession and spontaneous comment. Analyse them, split the stories into ever-smaller pieces.

To talk your way out of someone. Or feel your way out. To be locked out. Fall in, fall out. What else?

I don't want to make a list.

Signals reaching their destination. Resonance. I knew something. But exactly what I knew I don't know.

I know exactly where we were, the first time I drew certain conclusions. I had ignored signs I should have taken more seriously.

Night: I wake with an acute sense of longing. A new organ flutters and gapes inside me. I instinctively know that it is not made for movement. It must be still and mute as a liver.

Last night, with N . . . I had not imagined that we were alike in everything. But when I have seen us (but when have I ever seen us!) and thought about us, now and in the future, the feeling has always been that we dwell *within* something – a common life. A roomy coat, second-hand, impregnated with the mingled scents of our lives. Did I just invent that image? Is it true?

I saw an older man. Straight back, thick grey hair and long legs. Jeans. It could have been you thirty years from now. Walking away from me and coming back to me. Because that is where you belong.

Enough now. Don't bury it in writing. Don't do it. Don't try and make it better.

To be co-dependent in someone else's illness. Adjustment, self-censorship, one's own grief and hidden disappointment at not being the exception. The one who gets an ounce of warmth, a sense that there is a future-for-us.

To not be chosen and still believe that there is a 'we'. That is a time-limited hope. Someone says: only you can determine when the time is up.

Someone else says: he has to take care of this with his doctor and therapist. But he has to let you in. If he keeps you out it's hard to maintain the relationship, even in the short term.

I keep the relationship going in my mind. It's like the silence between two sentences. A dialogue illustrated with an abstract landscape. A pause. A distraction. A clarification?

You get well and break up with me.

You get well and come back to me.

But what does 'come back' mean? To renew the conversation, the kinship between words and skin?

You are just about present enough that I can still hope. Note that I don't use the word 'extinguish' about hope. *Spark, flame, turn on, turn off.* Those are not our words.

H says: Will N be able to forgive you for what you have seen?

H and I know that magical thinking is part of reality, and that we all to some degree invent each other. For psychotic people the rules are different, but no one is psychotic here.

To be out of touch to this degree, to give this little of oneself, is risky. Maybe he doesn't know that. Perhaps he should know that?

Who should wake whom, and bring them back to life? We wake ourselves. Wake up and act.

Was it a dream, that conversation about some steps leading up towards the light?

In theory, it's about hope. In real life that light is my child.

I am the only one who is unhappy in love. I am the only one who is grieving.

If he doesn't come back, he's an idiot. If he doesn't want me.

H says: 'I can verify that.'

I want to hold on to that word: verify. I tell him. I say I want it written down on paper, like a diploma. It's evidence. The verifiable.

I say: 'I want him to be well so I can kill him.'

H says: 'Yes, there is truth in that. Good plan. Kill him so he can be reborn.'

I say: 'But I am not angry with him. For the first time in my life, I don't want to draw conclusions. Because conclusions are about endings, and distance.'

H says: 'And that makes you vulnerable.'

I say: 'I'll have to see how long I can remain vulnerable without hurting too much.'

I tell H about the night in N's flat. The desolate feeling that he was right next to me in bed, and about to leave me. The fear. A predestined terror.

H says: 'But it wasn't yours. Not even yours. It's your mother. Your parents in you. But they don't really have all that much to do with you.'

> Johanna liked her psychoanalyst, H, and reading this I see the bond between them. *Yes, there is truth in that. Good plan. Kill him so he can be reborn.* So funny, and also so true. H reminds me of the realistic squire Jöns, the voice of sanity and common sense in Bergman's film *The Seventh Seal*. And he is right. Only some kind of break could have led to renewal.

The image of the man who has fallen asleep in front of the TV. It's on, but muted. The remote is in his hand.

He wakes up . . . and turns the TV off. I don't want it to end there. That sequence is us.

Everything you said we would do together. You wanted to do everything with me. If that's true, then why is it over?

The dream about the sweet animal biting me. Again! In the arm. The borderline between sucking and biting, pleasure and pain. The borderline between trust and uncertainty.

All those years of therapy, talking about feelings of homelessness, abandonment and desolation. And then to recognise all that in someone else – that was like coming home, a cure. And then: to really see it in him and to understand that I can't heal him, but that I still feel that *I* am cured, or at least that I am at home in my own story.

There is (I admit) a sense that you came so empty-handed to our relationship in terms of context and circumstances, but also that it was exactly that which made our love so pure. Language, skin, scent. That was what we had. It made our love safe. Everything else could come and go.

Christmas Eve, 2020. Morning. I look out on the street. It's empty. Not *empty* in the sense of one or two people milling about. When I look out on the street there's nobody there.

The difference between one and no one. I didn't know it was so big.

I dreamt about a foreign city. A journey, Christmas, early dusk. A cobblestone square, a Baroque church beyond. A lorry drives past, and on the back of it is a skinned lobster, as big as a whale. 'Lobster for New Year!' someone exclaims, delighted. 'And skinned and ready to eat!'

At first sight it's repulsive to me. The disgusting scales, parts, antennae, all those ungraspable details. Then I see that the lobster is breathing, the back heaving and subsiding, the eyes black dots. It makes no sound, and its eyes don't have the capacity to express feeling. But it's alive, even though it has been skinned and boiled. The pain and the silence. The torture and the stoicism. It is breathing on the smoke-grey lorry. I sink down to the ground and weep, sobbing in grief. One in our group, my friend's teenage daughter, taps me on the shoulder, tells me off. She says they have all been looking for me, and that the rental car is badly parked. I say they should have gone without me. They are in a hurry to get to a museum and they could have gone, they could have called me. I am not guilty; I don't want to be made to feel guilty about my sadness. Do your own thing. But how can we do our own thing when we are travelling in a group and every plan is agreed between all of us? How can it suddenly be acceptable that I step out of our togetherness, breaking our contract? What gives me that right? My sadness? The fact that I have seen something which only I can understand?

> The lobster's mute pain. I think of Johanna's reflections about N as the one who can't bear to be seen with love. Here's a reversal: N gets a shell, the lobster a skin. And Cullberg's words: the parts. 'The disgusting scales, parts, antennae, all those ungraspable details'.

> No more to say, and nothing to weep
>   for but the Beings in the Dream . . .
>   Allen Ginsberg, *Kaddish* (1961).

Today I don't remember us. I see no future. I don't long for you. I long to be comforted.

There's a black Christmas star at the gym.

The stale bread is thinking in the cupboard. So many secrets. Why didn't you tell me? I throw it out.

The little snowflakes dancing outside the window. There are always some which fly past and then come back and stop for a while. They want eye contact. I see them, but just when I begin to feel the connection, they reveal their lack of interest.

The faint scent of you. My nausea. (Eating, training, thinking, longing. Eating, training, thinking, longing, writing. Missing, missing, missing, missing, missing, writing.)

I write you messages of love, questions and observations, and send them to myself.

Let the tree outside my window be just a tree. Not a sign, a premonition, a warning.

I have never experienced anything like this.

Believe me.

I read about the first vaccinations in Sweden. Every time I see the word doctor – *läkare* – I read lover – *älskare*.

Unfair: I will never become as ill as you are. You will never miss me as I miss you.

The tin roofs, black, glossy, wet with rain. I watch them every morning and look at them again during the day. I always come back to the window. But today I notice notches in the tin. The roofs are striped. They are almost as obviously striped as they are black. What unknown thing am I seeing? What do I know that I can't account for?

I dream about my childhood home, my grandmother, Christmas. The electric Christmas candelabra is in the kitchen window; the TV is on in the dining room. There's the candlestick with three arms. By the dresser in the kitchen there are some wet footprints. Someone has trampled around in their boots, there's melted snow and gravel on the lino. Is there a criminal in the house, a thief, maybe a murderer? The man comes back into the kitchen. My grandmother can't see in the gloom, and she has removed her hearing aid. I hold her averagely cooperative body (always a bit too neutral). She does not respond to my hug. Says: 'It's not you, right?'

She doesn't believe it's me. She can't see me, feel me or hear me.

The tree is quiet. The branches are still. The snow swirls from the sky to the ground. Life is in violent movement, even when we can't see it.

Autoimmune diseases – how the body turns against itself.

Language unravels.

Empty consolations, dirt. Whatever has to be hidden. Whatever one wants to get away from. First it has to come out.

And my own shame: that I am too similar to the person I once was. The same useless light. The same look, trying to make some connection. But I am preoccupied with becoming. My grandmother's listless arms round my active body. 'It's not you, right?' As if there was a suspicion in the family that I am not me.

How do you fail, how do you bear the half-measures without glossing over them or becoming hysterical?

That washing line (neatly rolled up like a bundle of yarn, the last metre tied tightly round the middle), what did you have in mind to do with that?

But we hardly know each other. Or: we know each other despite the short period that we have . . . known each other. I want to say that we haven't seen each other for a while, but I can't, because it sounds too normal. Flat, or even provocative. For you, time is different, a blink and an incomprehensible effort. I hold my breath and think about the ants we saw on the path last summer. I wondered about their speed. Do they only have one gear? The dream about the lobster without its shell comes back. The encapsulated pain, the almost unnoticeable breathing. How time passes inside someone who is tormented and tired. Time heals. But you also have to heal time.

I dream that I am not believed and it makes me crazy. I say it again and again, and no one believes me. Someone laughs; someone else turns away. It doesn't matter what I'm saying – I am not someone who is trusted. I am all ages, but most of all I'm a child. I hide in a staircase, then kneel by a locked attic storage unit. I have torn off all my clothes in self-punishment and need for compassion, a wish that everyone will *see* with their own eyes that I am not lying or making up stories. In the middle of all those people I feel a sense of unreality emerging – my own state of being.

Nothing from you yesterday. Greater chance of a message today, which makes it a stronger day. Today is like a thigh muscle, long, strong and smooth. Not very sensitive.

Last night I escaped from a prison. I had to be fast, and yet I took the time to calculate distances and effort. From the gate across the muddy yard, up on the car roof, then over the wall and cross the lock by the river; through the woods into the market, pass the taxis by the town gate, and then into town. Become invisible on the busiest streets. Disappear into the crowd.

My grandmother went on coach trips with the Housewives' Association. Imagine that. A society for housewives.

If not Covid – then I would be in Sussex with my friend in that house. The meadows; the skies. To be left alone but still be together, not too sad, not too distant. The care, the gaze. *Permission. To be permitted.*

My own journey. Away from you.

Last night we spoke on the phone. The voice is yours, but the rest? You are coming back. But will you come back to me? It will take time. Who will I be, by then?

I have to stop mixing us up.

I wake up screaming. 'Help! Help! Help me!' I am in the living room of my childhood home, screaming so violently that I can see the soundwaves as light-yellow threads over the fields and through the woods.

Someone knocked on the door, someone else opened it. Outside was a stranger, with a parcel. I tore off the paper (white with green and red stars, insipid). Inside was a book with a dedication both on the title page and on the last page. I didn't read them. I knew the harm was done – it was a spell. The only spell in the world that has the power to annihilate.

A spell. Sorcery? For the first time I wonder if there is anything in you that is actually harmful to me.

Only I can determine when this becomes unbearable. But first I have to come to that realisation.

Despair can make itself known like this: every internal organ is suddenly surrounded by a shining net of blackness. The body is black and inside it the organs hang close together, isolated in their own nets, their own languages. They are luminous like planets. It's beautiful but there's no point trying to understand it. I stare at it until I'm blind.

I knelt down at the gym with the bar over my shoulders. For a few seconds I saw black. I submitted.

My ex-husband says there is a certain kind of sadness which makes you good with children.

A certain kind of sadness makes me methodical about taking down the Christmas decorations.

And about writing.

Your cheek is mine when I touch it. Your face is more mine than my own hand. Is that beautiful or repulsive?

I shy away from responsibility. I kneel down, weeping. Am I small enough now? Big enough not to demand too much.

Nutshell
golden eyeshadow
insignificant
hide it, hide it for later.

BOOK 6: JANUARY–MARCH 2021

I am ashamed of the great expectations I had as a young adult. Ashamed of my big words and mediocre craftsmanship. Ashamed of my hubris. But when I was a child, it saved me.

I dreamt about a frozen corpse in one of those blue boxes filled with sand for icy roads in winter. The most striking detail: the hollowed-out chest in the frosty-white hard sand. The box is next to a gate leading to a palace garden. It is night. I turn my back in the dream or in my bed trying to sleep through the night, the stench of the corpse slowly emanating from the box. I don't understand why I didn't move. Didn't I have the energy, or did I need to be near the accident?

In the garden there is a border of brightly coloured flowers. The artificial light makes them look unreal at night. I stand looking at them with a few friends. We see them in very different ways. One person sees only black and white. Another feels that the flowers are almost colourless, with some elements of purple. I see them sparkling with colour, but I also see something else: a woolly hat and mittens in the border, red angora against black earth. I am the only one who can see them, and they come and go. Visible, invisible.

> The dream turns into the anguished experience of not being believed, a recurrent theme in Johanna's dreams. What is it that we don't believe? What has happened? In the dream she sees things others can't see. I think about sanded roads in winter (safe streaks of yellow sand on black ice), angora rabbits, childhood, a murder victim.
>
> But what do the mittens and woolly hat, invisible to the others, mean?

Are they a clue to who has murdered the man in the sand box, or is there another victim? You don't believe me? Something crawls across my throat. But is that too just my imagination? I start so violently that I wake up.

> In her novel *A Fictional Diary* Johanna writes about memories frozen in ice:

'I see a face. Some berries. Raspberries, sour cherries, faintly transparent. An apricot, the stone a foetus in the womb. A hand, a Madonna gesture; protective, inviting, fingertips turning white. Frost on the skin. A leathery chicken claw, sharp as a kitchen tool. A book with stiff pages. Notes in blue ink. Ink stains, yellow on the edges, spread like bruises.'
Is the frozen body a distorted memory? But the strongest feeling in the dream is the frustration, almost panic, about not being believed. Perhaps the signals from the unconscious (to do with a dead body, exhaustion and distorted vision) were too dramatic and strange to be believable. Perhaps Johanna is the one who doesn't believe, and also the one panicking because she is not believed.

The absurdity of this? I am valiant as a soldier. Book in hand, lump in my throat, acidic anxiety in my stomach. I sit motionless at my post. On the surface I am immovable. I am on duty. At times I don't breathe deeply enough and get a few seconds of vertigo. The book I am reading is about longing for home and longing to get away. A moment ago, I had a taste of coffee and bread in my mouth. Now I feel my teeth clenching.

And you? Are you walking the streets and roads of your town? Has the snow been cleared, are the streets sanded? Is it icy? I guess that's all. That you walk those streets. And I sit here. I know there is a small opportunity for humour here, an angle that might bring liberating laughter. But it passes me by.

School days it's still like getting up at night. Only a few windows are lit up – people's bedrooms face the yards, not the street. The man in the yellow vest and jacket is by his kiosk, opening the day. He greets a woman passing by with her dog. Is he smoking?

This loneliness must not be fixed or taken away from me.

I have rolled the bar over my knees until they are blue and swollen. Is that a blue tit I hear through the noise of the snowplough? I look at my knees and see the blue tit. Same colours: yellow, yellow-green, blue-green, blue.

The kiosk man puts out a table and two chairs. They are always there, but I have never seen him put them out before. Now he's smoking, leaning against a dark wall between two illuminated advertising boards.

Something new has to happen with this body. Something that is not back pain or blue-tit knees.

There are still Christmas stars in the windows, though it's almost February. White shapes, sharp. Cuts in the dark. I think of cartoons of bangs or explosions. The stars don't twinkle, they claw.

Mornings I'm in my place by the window. The dark, the candle, coffee. I go from dreams to this. I appear. Sometimes I imagine you so vividly, how quietly you sleep, knees pressed together, the weight of your hands. The relationship between your skin and the sheets. Like seeing the nakedness of a face in a passing train. And afterwards a greater loneliness.

Today the coffee tastes metallic, my body is an old waffle, my skin someone else's. Not even my veins are familiar to me. But is there not a certain freedom in being a temporary stranger to oneself? Someone you glimpse out of the corner of your eye without wanting to have much to do with them?

Alpine mini-landscapes on the gutter opposite, lit from the street, hard shadows against the roof. People ski off-piste there, picnic, die in avalanches. Someone makes breakfast for their family in a chalet. Someone steps out to the porch and wants to walk away, never to come back. Or just to go for a walk before sunrise.

I am here at dawn every morning to make sure my body doesn't leave me. To guard it, not disregard it as I did when I was younger. My trick, my strategy.

The pencil against paper, a ritual, an immune reaction, a barrier. The trees don't shake off the layer of snow even though it's thicker than some of the branches. No, it just looks like that. The snow shrouds the trees.

I think about my friends, how they wake up, get out of bed. Their sleepy bodies, remnants of dreams flaring up, disappearing. I move in the sphere of their warmth. A true protection.

I generate hope. It's like a potion under the skin. Today I am empty. Empty of feelings, thoughts and movement. The loss of meaning – it's not an atmosphere, it's more like a crack in the painting. It's not your fault. I have felt like this as far back as I can remember. Sometimes I wish I could exaggerate the feeling; widen the crack.

You would catch up with me, bring me to a halt, put your hand over my forehead, fell me to the ground. Turn me round. Would you? That?

I have moved the chair a few centimetres. Now I sit at a right angle to the corner of the house opposite. I straddle the façade.

A friend said: you have to creatively remake the relationship.

There is an edge of snow in the gutter, pleated like the edge of a tart. No, like a shell. A flounce, a stiffened wave.

The fantasy of a miracle. Not a miracle I would experience, but rather that *I* would be someone's miracle.

My childish hope that I would be the answer to someone's question.

A crawling sense of resistance, not just in the muscles but also in the air surrounding the skin, as though invisible molecules had gathered to create a certain kind of pressure. In every movement I make there is an alternative immobility. But still, I overcome it. I make the bed. Not just carelessly, but properly, as if liberating myself from the resistance. Come out on the other side. I straighten the sheet, remove a crumb, fit the duvet in the corner of the duvet cover, shake it out. Then I take a shower and wash my hair, finishing with a cold shower.

I am thinking about the concept of metal fatigue, material fatigue. When the molecules deep inside a thing are no longer quite aligned. The dry rubber band, the shapeless old jumper, the metal that suddenly breaks. Something solid has changed and become brittle, but you can't tell from the surface.

Every laborious movement emerges from a deep resistance. My body moves against a membrane, a gel. The mute hand of emptiness.

I put on Depeche Mode, pretend-smoking a slim cigarette. Lip gloss carelessly applied; scent sprayed over my head. Atmospheric life hacks. But really, I don't have the energy to dance. My body is heavy, sleeping, I have fallen asleep like a child carried in a sling inside my own clothes.

A small child inside the adult clothes and body. A child pretending to be a teenager. Disco girl. A little girl who becomes paralysed with fear of the almost hallucinatory lollipop at Skansen, who tames her fear of alienation by experimenting with lip gloss and pretend-smoking. Life hacks. Scenes, tricks, shortcuts through existence.

The day after Margareta's memorial in February 2022 we went shopping at the Harrods of Stockholm, NK. An ironic life hack to make us feel gleeful and free, *feminine* in that way which is both authentic and a playful performance; a game with the man behind the counter who let Johanna test scent after scent, who talked layers and brands, who genuinely laughed with us.

A life hack – away from the memorial and Johanna's melanoma of the eye.

But in the notebooks we are not there yet. Now it's January 2021, seven or eight months before the diagnosis.

I dreamt that we lived in a small US settlement by an airstrip. An airbase, I think. You had just become a certified pilot. The sky was mute, a cool grey-blue. The houses were low, dirt-coloured. I wanted you to loop the loop and make a heart in the air for me. But then I thought it was too dangerous and asked you not to do it.

I dreamt about a boat in the Stockholm archipelago, about islands and a dark-blue sea. The wind changed the surface of the water from still to matt and furrowed. Suddenly the captain jumped off the moving boat, and I was left on board alone. I had to steer and didn't know how to stop the boat or even how to slow it down. I stood by the helm and looked down into the transparent water. I could see the bottom and all the things there – stones, seaweed, the wheel of a bicycle, an aluminium stepladder. In between were stretches of sand, flat or serrated into ridges. But the fact that I saw the bottom of the sea didn't help me to judge the depth. Would we go aground against a rock, or would we sink or get stuck in the sand and maybe capsize?

My vision did not help me. But vision was all I had. I couldn't take my eyes off the depths in order to find the button or the lever to turn off the engine. The bottom shimmered in nuances of green and yellow and grey.

The last sentence in this paragraph has been crossed out: 'There were elements of rusty red in the sand.'

I dreamt that I, or maybe we, dropped a glass. It didn't break. Another glass fell to the floor. Was it cracked, or was that line a single hair? Or was it a crack as fine as a single hair? I felt the glass with my thumb, and it moved. So it was a hair. Or was it a crack that could move? As long as I touched the crack the glass remained whole.

The dream about the crack was a storm petrel. Now I drop things, my scissors get stuck in sticky tape, I fumble with the sleeve of my dressing gown, I spill coffee powder on the counter, my neck stiffens up, I can't get the drawer to close.

I look at my hands. They are frozen. My fingers are coarse and stiff. I don't want this. My body is on strike. My intuition is at a dead end. It's as though a curse has been poured into the flat in the sharp morning light. I have shooting pains in my neck, my body parts belong to someone who is dead. My brain struggles against the wind. Says, clean that up, wet some kitchen roll, put the flat of your hand under the counter, catch the coffee powder and throw it in the bin, with the paper.

My skin itches. I have tears in my eyes. These words are written as one, not apart. My brain says, get it all done now, and then you can have coffee and porridge by the kitchen window. The brain says, I don't know why everything suddenly became so insurmountable.

On this day. Everything breaks, cracks, turns inside out. If I touch my arm, I will cut myself. I pick an orange out of the bowl and my thumb goes straight through it. It looked whole, but it's rotten. I throw it in the bin, miss, make a mess.

A thumb through the fontanelle.

The boundaries are eradicated.

A hair in my mouth. A crack. What's it like to say that. To hear it. To write it. To read it.

What is it like to read it.

The room falls silent, I am sitting still at my desk.

The mute panic of the body.

'The bottom shimmered in nuances of green and yellow and grey. ~~There were elements of rusty red in the sand.~~'

The body tries to speak but Johanna crosses out the most important clue: rusty red like *blood*, something biological, therefore, something that is growing; something she *sees*, therefore something to do with vision, with her eye.

The body was speaking, but she didn't hear it.

Everything and/or nothing is populated and imbued with being: things, body, birds, the mortar on the façade opposite, the melting ridges of snow, the tree, the words, the balls of dust, the electric cords, the flecks of skin stuck in the blanket, the candle wax that dripped and stiffened on the windowsill. Everything is dead and/or alive. The clouds.

The thought is untenable, it cuts the body into pieces from the inside. The body and/or the thought. The self-image, the self of the image. Close your eyes to every reflective surface.

I speak to one friend, then to another. I speak to friends who love you. It all comes to life. Understanding, explanations, theories. Then the near future and the not so near future. And the word 'then' becomes a tentative link, a little bridge of tenderness. In the end you are so present that I don't even have to think about you. You sit with us, and then we talk about other things. But when I get home, you are no longer with me. And the contrast between conjuring you up and then losing you is as hard as slipping on ice and hitting the back of one's head. As hard as being tricked. 'You should see your face now!' someone laughs.

The liquid that runs out of my eyes is not tears. It's bile. It's a thinner liquid, almost unnoticeable. It itches.

Everything was open, free and false. I knew that I would rot and then die but I wanted to dry out and then die. I knew that I would glitter with some quality of assertiveness and determination. It was the only offer. It was a burden to know that as a young girl, a young woman.

Fuck it. It's over now. The only ingredient that remains in part is loneliness. It's the organ in which the images arise.

Nothing is more real than these pencilled words. I can't leave them other than for short breaks. They wait for me in a room or in a corner. Nothing is more alive. They fill the flat: a small lung, breathing. A minor circulatory system, blood pulsing, hissing, whispering. When I am with the pencilled words I am at home. When I put down my pencil I'm outside, in a steep and vertiginous landscape where it's hard to judge distances. The words wait, unwritten.

Friends. The lonely people with the warm voices. As though they have come very close to reality and treat it with respect.

Is there a solution now? For you/us? My back and neck ache and stiffen, my shoulders are frozen, compacted. Frozen earth. It's almost impossible to imagine that anything could grow there.

I dream that we are the same or that we see the same thing. Body and face smiling towards the sun. The greenery behind. The darkness in the greenery. A suction, inwards. Or an ambush. A darkness that could spread. But the body keeps it at bay, as if (completely unconsciously) concealing or resisting another narrative.

It's a daydream. I wouldn't dream like this at night, about us, would I? No, the daydreams are always the ones that are out of control. The night knows something else.

My eyelashes touch the top branches of the tree. The pigeons fly, like the pupils of eyes. Some misapprehension has been going on for the last few days. It's light outside, I turn off the lights. There are no answers in me.

I slept as though I were digging, burying myself in the ground. Woke up stiff with a flaming headache. I remember the dream I had soon after giving birth. The small child in the yard; its naked, downy skull covered in earth. It pressed itself down between the paving stones, down into the earth. Said: Do not follow me.

The headache – a column – astonishing. A pillar of salt behind the eye. My vision. I am aware of it, but I hide it in my body. I resist it and make it worse; I enter into the pain until it cuts and burns.

There is always a part of me that doesn't understand pain. That believes there is some kind of alleviation in the eye of the storm. A little clearing where the animals can sleep. A mild place patrolled by insanity, by an enormous movement.

To cut one's way to tenderness. Fall asleep in a snowdrift and trust that it's a wave carrying me to shore. It goes too fast, too slowly.

I dream that there are snakes in the grass. That you say I am a coward. Not because I would lie but because I wouldn't the truth.

> *Because I wouldn't the truth?* Is there denial even in the grammar, as though Johanna can't bear to write that she doesn't want to see the truth, or own the truth, or tell the truth?

Or am I reading too much into the text?

Am I lacking in care?

Johanna, say.

Johanna.

All my words mean only one thing: I miss you.

My world is different now. I am trying to think about this catastrophe, an illness that felt like an accident.

I try to control myself, but at times I cry until I shake. It doesn't matter what I think or write. Your absence remains.

Suddenly you are there. *I know*, you say.

I hear you say it.

I know.

Do you remember that last week when we talked about how to answer the words *I love you?*

Just say, *I know*, you said and smiled, and I understood that there is no debt in love. It's a state of mind, not a gift. A state of grace. It's enough to smile, and say *I know*.

I see you smile.
I see you fade away.
Johanna.

The sun shines through the open window straight into my cup of coffee. The steam from the cup seems to radiate back. The bakery cart with deliveries for the café opposite rattles its beat on the pavement. Birdsong – is it the blue tit?

Now the day wakes, the child, hunger. Time wakes and winds itself up in the rhythm of the street, of all the streets.

I got sick and for the first time (really?) I understood just how ill it's possible to be, without dying. I talked to my dear godmother. I told her how much she meant to me and she said that she was so very fond of me, too. I guessed as much, I said. But it's nice not to have to keep guessing. For the first time in my life, I long to be a child, to come into the kitchen and see my mother there. See my godmother, my grandmother. To know that they exist.

I see the garden and the darkness under the shrubs. That's enough.

I long for early morning when everyone is asleep

and the sea is still and blank. Silence in the mouth and birds flying low. The cool of the night lingering in the bramble.

I long to share that, not to share myself (perhaps that was a misunderstanding). To stand together, sniffing the air. I know, it's only about brief moments. Clarifying moments. But I want to be there. Because it's incomparable. The landscape by the sea, the rail of the balcony in Tel Aviv. The market about to open. The magnolia in London! The chill in the bramble. I can see it. My daughter sleeps. Her scent as she sleeps is that of a small child.

Live! Just live. I don't want to long for it. I just want to live. But to really live you have to also long for something, isn't that so?

A seagull flies by; it wraps its wings round my cheeks. The feathers are cool from the wind but the body inside is warm. I cry and the tears are a relief.

The snow has melted. The roofs are dry and matt. The tin could be rubber.

And then a heron.

I'm almost sure it was a heron.

BOOK 7: MARCH–MAY 2021

The windowpanes – *fönsterrutorna* – are streaky in the spring light. Everything is bright and dirty. There is space for a whole world behind my teeth. In the next block is a spreading savannah, burnt grass, smooth paths. Plastic bottles roll soundlessly across the ground. The wind comes from the sea. Open, desolate fields. I just walk and walk until someone pulls down the backdrop, says, 'That's enough for today.'

I go back, misread: the conditions – *förutsättningarna* – are streaky in the spring light.

There are flecks of blue in me, like the depths of the sea marked on a map. Dark-blue graves. Light oval fields stretch from my breast, diagonally. They remind me of lungs. Childish movements without childhood.

I make coffee, hurry back to the window. What was it I didn't want to miss? A lost word? A sensation of love? Something snuck out. I sit wide awake at my post, and everything runs through my fingers.

Sand, eternity, symbolism. Confetti . . . everything and nothing.

I still don't dare to think about the dream. The small child. I held it, then dropped it. Its teeth were knocked out or pushed into the jaw. The child's inability to express pain. A real injury, unexpressed. Impossible, impossible to think, to carry the burden of guilt. A responsibility without response.

My brother, my child, my beloved, my mute and broken mother.
    Whose name am I?

The voice heals me. In the dark, forehead to forehead. There is a similarity between you and me, stretching out like a bright shadow. I think about that now, watching the dirty shimmer of the pavement below. How the world gets in through the eyes.

The acts of a whole day. No one named, no one forgotten. Layers of similarity, of the right things. I have never understood it before as I understand it now. The clasp of a hand, movements, broken-off sentences, solicitude. Careless, exaggerated, never enough and enough until I hear a sound from the turned-off mobile, words from the sleeping mouth. Almost unnoticeably, concepts break down. A little sandpit of insanity. Perhaps it's called bedtime. But the I which may not exist is still made manifest here, a hacking machinery inside the doll.

The windows in the façade opposite are all wearing eyeshadow, carelessly applied. 'Zing!' A black bird with unrealistically short wings flies past me, but it's just the sun making the wingtips transparent. It's the magpie. The kiosk man has hosed down the pavement. A lorry reverses, beeping. Suddenly I notice the scent of cut flowers from the florist. Light green and light white.

M at the gym tells me I have a strong frontal bone. I am a bear, an ox. When I gave birth the father of the child said I was a warrior. It was so nice, that word. I can flex my body, lock the effort. Then it's encapsulated in the torso, but it's also everywhere and I am it. If I close my eyes there is only the effort, the force, but that is nothing. A ball of darkness. As though in the deepest space inside the body there is an outside.

Spring ice. Between winter and warmth.

People fall in and die. The ice moans and sings. The crystals don't cohere.

I see a human being standing on an organ, balancing in a thunder of notes. The body meets death halfway. The crystals don't cohere.

I was fascinated by meteorites when I was a child. To be one. To come from far away and make a dent on earth. But in my imagination the meteorite could take off again, and travel around the world. At night it would come rolling back to lie down close to the body of a house or to a body.

The houses opposite are quiet, a layer of sleep in the façade. A seagull glides over the roof and then seems to be projected backwards on film. There are hints of swelling buds on the chestnut tree. And through that vision, another: the sea, the bare slope, the brambles, the sky, the sky.

I am a child, I walk alone on a dirt road. The ploughed fields, the stream. The edge of the forest, the clumps of trees. The sound of running water in the ditch. I am in the exact mood-point between longing and waiting. A word that doesn't exist.

A blackbird in profile on the chestnut branch. On this day it is a flying hole between the houses.

There are not enough ingredients in the days. I can't think what's lacking. Great holes in the cake. Guesses. A mute procession.

A seagull flies along the second floor of the block, then a little higher, up to the third floor. It looks heavier when it flies low.

Someone who opens their strong arms or their weak arms. Who opens a hand or an eye. Someone who encloses me or closes up. Arms stretched forwards or a shoulder blade jutting out.

I remember the time when I could say anything to you, as though speech was a paper plane soaring and cutting through air that was glass and cream, our intuitions. (If we can't return to that place, we no longer exist.)

What's on offer today? Long strides in syrup, the steam from the coffee curls up like someone's hair. A singer. The diagonal stomach muscles tighten. The origin falls apart. It's as it should be. At the bakery they are selling challah with or without seeds.

I am weaving a morning with the help of phrases and musculature.

In the tree, a little grey knuckle. It must be a bird. Not just a cut-off branch, a knot in the bark. Let it be a little bird. Let me know and be right throughout this day.

The massage oil has dusty shoulders. The blackbird is a hole with a beak. The beak is a flap you pull. Then the hole disappears, and you are back in unreality.

I dreamt that an estate agent called to say he's found a studio apartment in Paris. The price was almost nothing. It was as if made for me: big windows and rooms, a view towards a canal and a boulevard. But I felt that I had become old and told him that I didn't want it. That I wanted to be in a place where I understood the language. The agent insisted, describing the plane trees outside and the floor plan. I said: 'I don't even understand your language.'

I woke at five, speedy and anxious. Something about this hollowed-out day had already failed.

We would kiss all the time and turn towards each other. You would put a loaf of bread on my head. We would point out the place outside the shop next door where you first took me in your arms. An acquaintance passed us by on the street and I decided I would never get to know him.

I want to travel and to carve love into my body. Like childhood pain or fate. Or to travel and to carve it out of me. To come home, and not remember.

It's so hard for women to believe in their own imprint on life. It's so easy to make yourself needed, like a little hook catching love. You think it will lead to guarantees, to durability, but it can just as easily lead to rage.

The fantasies keep you alive. The fantasies push you against the edges. Here, deep in the brain, is a sandy hollow, as smooth and open as an indentation made by a metal ball in sand or the fall of a meteorite.

You are making progress. You speak and your voice effortlessly penetrates the skin and calms me. But something also falls backwards within me. The electricity is suddenly cut and it's pitch-black, impossible to orientate myself.

A man pushes a handcart with a wooden box from the bakery to the café down the street. In the dim light inside the box: rows of cream cakes. When the wheels bounce against the pavement the cakes touch each other; imprints of whipped cream. Tiny silly kisses on a shoulder.

I dreamt about a street wet with rain on the edge of a city. Chestnut trees, heavy and secret with white flowers. The trunks were stained by the rain, inviting. 'I want a tree like that to be my mother,' I said to the man walking next to me. 'What do you mean?' he asked. 'Your meaning is elusive.' He took my hand and held it tight. I said, 'We don't know each other. That's why we are so close. There is nothing between us.' He said, 'It's only now, before we know anything, and then later when we know almost everything, that closeness actually exists.'

I woke up and felt tired. Now I am thinking about that tree. The trunk. The darkness in the greenery. Can't summer come soon so the dreams can escape?

A memory of a children's book, a typical 1970s real-life story. A little boy in South America pulls a plough with his buffalo. The plough sinks into the mud and something terrible comes out of it. A volcano. Not from a mountain, but straight from the earth. I was not sure it was true. And precisely that uncertainty made the image all the stronger. That wound under the surface. A roar straight through the order of life itself.

Terrible thoughts: needles causing invisible harm. Penetrating the skin, moving inside the body, skidding, puncturing. An internal wound, the kind one is not aware of, disfiguring, distorting, weakening.

> Johanna associates 'to not be given access to love' when she reflects on her compulsive thoughts about needles, but I think about her liver biopsy a year later – not one long needle deep inside the liver, but two. 'Not for amateurs,' she said, making light of it.
>
> I think of the port in her arm where a nurse injected morphine and anti-nausea and anti-anxiety medication, one shot after the other. Johanna, almost unconscious, moaned slightly, and the nurse – neutral, matter-of-fact – said that it probably hurt when the skin tightened with all the fluids.
>
> The unconscious cruelty of care.
>
> Why inflict pain on dying patients?

My godmother exists as a being inside me. Her wisdom, her patience, her humanity. Her singularity in me. It's secret.

I wait but it isn't obvious that I wait. I wait and it's obvious that I wait. I do things while I wait. I read and think, I talk to friends. I write. And all the time I am waiting. When will I be done waiting? When I don't need to wait any longer?

What does waiting look like in relation to longing?

April weather. A pigeon flies through the snowfall. The snow looks like it came from two sacks, emptied and shaken out. It whirls around like in an old film. Five pigeons through the snowfall.

> Johanna dreams that a horse pushes her against the wall, biting and kicking her. No one comes to help, and she has to hurt the horse to free herself.
> She dreams that she looks at her body, at muscles that have turned to fat, a blue network of veins under the skin. She walks towards Skeppsholmen and overhears a man say about the Tivoli at Gröna Lund: 'I only did the free fall once. I did not enjoy that. I was as scared afterwards as I was during the fall.'
> Every now and then she sees N. His depression has abated somewhat, but

he is not able to maintain close contact.
Johanna waits, controls herself, writes.
The diagnosis is still some months in the
future.

I dream about beauty, about scents, eyeshadow, creams,
serums. I take great pleasure in looking at lipsticks in
a cool range of colours, lip gloss and lots of pigments.
But when a salesperson tells me about an offer on
facials and says, 'You have to take care of yourself, it's
your duty,' I feel sad and leave.

Down by Årstaviken I pass a couple in their thirties.
The sun is behind me, in their eyes. She closes her eyes
and allows herself to be led by him. I see it over and
over like a sequence in a film. How she allows herself
to be led by him. The sun on her face, his arm round
her shoulders.

Johanna dreams about an unknown
lake, a city, a paved path. N takes down
laundry from a washing line and packs
it in a suitcase. There is not much time.
Something sexual happens between
them in a bed but the mood dissipates
and turns bleak:

A grey light, no shadows . . . There is something so flat about the scenes, one after the other. They are unanchored, fleeting. We can't reach each other. I wake up and feel as though my body has no muscles. The light is as flat and humourless as in the dream.

Thoughts: Stop eating. Cut yourself with the kitchen knife. No big deal, just a little scratch on the upper left arm. Stop being so strong. Don't go to the gym. Sleep longer. Be exhausted and let the hours pass. Dial down the expectations, dial down the effort. Dampen the emotions, flatten existence. Have a body that desires very little. Baby food, thin wafers, weak coffee. Don't cry. Instead, dip your fingertips in salt. Become a convalescent outside time.

On April 13th, 2021, precisely a year before she died, N came back and Johanna discovered that she missed writing about grief, waiting and longing. 'Now that you are here there are no words for us on paper. Those words are between us,' she writes.

She dreams about minding a small child. He gets hold of some pens and starts drawing on the walls of her mother's study. 'He has drawn all over, on walls, chairs, on the floor and knee height. Black, purple, yellow, turquoise.' Margareta radiates silent reprimands and criticism. Johanna cups her hand round the child's head, worried that he will lose his balance: 'His unsteadiness makes me dizzy. Mum looks at us as if wanting to say that her love is not unconditional.'

'It's the action that counts, but sometimes there is virtue in waiting. Today I wait for you even though you are here. A habit suddenly hard to break. A word from childhood comes back to me: mischief. My inactivity now is a passive form of mischief . . .'

Årstaviken was full of flamingos. The sun observed itself in the mirror of the peat-brown water. The birds were quietly floating around, absent, solitary and content.

They were the pale buoys. Almost white by the water, pink above.

It's a game, almost unconscious.

I have to remember that this period of illness will not shape us. The fact that I do all the cooking and

take care of everything practical. That I am a constant.
A carer.

When will you say:
    I want . . .
    I wish . . .
    I hope . . .
    I long for . . .

When will you say:
    You . . .
    Yourself . . .
    Yours . . .
    Us . . .
    Our . . .
    We . . .
    When will you say my name and that you love
me?

I sent you a text yesterday: 'Woke up and longed for
you.' You didn't answer. I know, you have no centre to
answer from. And you may not miss me. Perhaps you
feel some sort of need for me, or perhaps you feel that
you have to keep us going in the expectation that you
might miss me in the future. I should imagine that most
of all you long for the capacity to long for anything at

all. And that when I text you it doesn't light up your soul or fill you with a sense of mutual longing (like it used to, or at least I think so?). Perhaps you sense, instead, your own incapacity and loss. My longing, the fact that I miss you, might feel like a demand, or perhaps even a mockery? Asymmetry and guilt. Yes, I understand that. I should have known better, and at the same time I have to do what I do, maintain my own sense of self. I long for you. I express that. I express myself. But is the result destructive? Am I wrecking something? There is a risk that what we have dries out, is pulverised . . . or that something (else) is simply revealed?

A thought (from time to time): you would like to love me. But you don't love me. You would like it to be us forever. But you can't maintain a 'we'. And you don't have the energy to think in terms of time. I carry our relationship. You don't, or at least you carry a very small part of it (even though you do visit). When you get better, you'll carry it too. You are afraid of it, and you have forgotten that if you love someone you carry the responsibility automatically. Carrying is implicit in love. And yes, it's about a particular weight and responsibility but it's not about guilt. I have no idea if you understand any of this, or if you are even ready to think about 'us'.

I wake up without any sense of longing, without any needs or wishes. No sense of sadness or anxiety. The sun rises higher above the roofs opposite now. The lime tree down the street, if it is a lime, is about to come into leaf. The church bells ring, it's 8 a.m. A bluesy sound.

Late April, and it's snowing. The lime which may be a maple lights up the street, green merging into yellow. An epiphany: the snow whirls around in every direction. Vertical streaks cross horizontal ones and there's a constant snowing upwards. Suddenly I understand that this is what the wind looks like: the snowflakes make the wind visible. Like language makes thoughts visible.

To come back to the window and my notes, and to never feel that they are without value. It is something. At least it is something. And when the 'real' text is written and it's terrible, not usable even in fragments, then I come back to the window and these notebooks and I try to make sure that it will come to something. That at the very least I am taking care of something. Fencing it, ringing it, catching it, and letting it go. Whatever is left is a trace of my identity on paper and a wish that it be shared, taken apart and made permeable by a reader. You.

Language is born from language. But everything else can break apart. Language at most takes a break or starts repeating itself. Sometimes it refuses to be written down.

I pay with time, mistrust, lethargy, a kind of dirty impatience, itchy envy. Not envy of those who write, but of those who write and still live their lives. Those (writers) who grow plants, pickle cucumbers, make their own sauerkraut and sourdough. Those who walk for hours, bringing coffee in a thermos. What I do, at least today and in the last week or weeks, is to be fully occupied with my non-writing. Interrupted by some paragraphs of printed-out text which later has to be deleted because it's too bad, dead on the page. It makes an impact for the first and last time in that laptop sound of emptying the bin. What is that? It sounds as though the document was both cancelled and burnt. As if I had written it on baking paper or dry leaves.

I am thinking about the Sibyl in Cumae outside Naples. She sat in the opening of the cave and arranged leaves in patterns from which it was possible to predict the future. A prophet about to be discovered. Then there was a gust of wind from the sea, and the divinations came to nothing. Did the leaves frazzle and rustle like the emptying of the laptop bin? I imagine the leaves of plane trees, leathery skins on the ground. The smile of the Sibyl as the wind shuffled her cards. Patient, all-knowing, or malicious and triumphant? For who knows on whose side the wind was?

Inspiration falters.

I wake up trembling. The spoor. The hint of something. That feeling of knowledge not yet cracked. The path leading to the sea. The opening. A fact. But apparently not yet. I caught a glimpse of something just now but got distracted and lost sight of it. The most difficult thing: to be still. I feel undressed, vulnerable, insistent.

Loneliness, and what surrounds it. Here it is. Shadows on the wall, the light in the corner. My silent breaths interrupted by a sigh, a yawn. Here I am. Soon I'll get up. Here is loneliness.

Every day I lose the thread. If I put it into words, the lost thread becomes the thread. I reach back into time. Whatever I don't see makes itself visible again if only I wait. I don't conceal the fact that I am waiting.

Dreamt about my mother. She was younger, beautiful, clean. Naked in bed, on white sheets. Her weak shoulders, heavy breasts, black hair. 'I am dying,' she said. 'Are you dying right now?' I asked. 'No, not right now,' she said, with her ringing loud laugh. Then suddenly she rolled over to her side and made some faltering movements. She lacked the muscular strength to keep herself upright. The movements were frightening, hopeless, pointless.

Write about the shadows, the photographs of shadows. Catch? No, not that word. Confirm, perhaps, or just accept. The loneliness, the silence of the shadows. And how much I like this stillness, the loneliness.

May 6th, 2021. My fifty-first birthday. My godmother, who is ninety-two, calls and tells me that she picked a bunch of violets for me the day I was born. My zero birthday. 'Does it feel like a long time ago?' I ask. 'No,' she says. 'It feels so recent. But still, it's your whole life. Such a long life for you and such a short time for me.' She tells me that she feels lonely in her memories. She remembers a time before the Second World War. And she feels lonely in other ways, too. And yet I don't see her as lonely. Why? Because to me she is so alive, so present, so honest in her way of being.

Mum, who can't speak, interrupts me when I tell her about this and that. 'Thank you for coming,' she finally says. I ask if she means 'coming' as in visiting her at the home, or as in coming into this world. Or both? She looks at me and I understand that she means both, and I feel so content that I carry on chatting, too shy to stay in the love and understanding between us.

To be able to write a book you have to write another one at the same time.

This is the book I am not writing. This text, which started out in pencil but is now often written in ink (but never on the laptop, always in the notebooks), is that book. It's the important one (for me), and therefore the secret one (for me too).

I dream that I am going to write a synopsis for a thriller. I can't do it. I'm recording a pilot where I play the lead, a man in a white linen suit and a blood-stained shirt, drops of blood on my trousers. I act badly and the blood looks fake, too light, too diluted.

I dream about a horse trying to bite me. Its heavy, insistent head. I try to keep it away, pushing against the muzzle. No good. If I hurt it, it will want to bite me even more. S is there and calms the horse down. I want her to remove it, to make it go away. She says I have to wait until it has calmed down. She understands something about horses that I don't, has access to something I don't. I don't just want it to be kind. I want it to go. I don't trust it. S does, because she knows it. I don't. I won't ever trust it.

Layers of sound, harmonising with layers of green. Foreground: the cooing of the pigeons. Background: the sound of the blackbirds. Between them is the hum of distant traffic, the odd car in the street below and the cries of the seagulls. The trees are lit up, the greenery transparent. A boy calls out, 'Dad, look at the pigeons!' The kiosk man hasn't opened up yet, the shutters are closed.

I write that your stilted text made me sad and that I am more vulnerable than I seem. You answer that you haven't yet found your way back to language.

I have pulled a muscle in my back, between the shoulder blade and the neck.

The beat of the pigeons' wings feels suddenly so close, as though someone was shaking a blanket out of the window. The cool morning air after rain. The pandemic, abating.

Two people greet each other on the street. Ringing laughter.

The coffee was borderline too weak.

It's true what S said yesterday: sometimes it's good *not* to remember dreams.

BOOK 8: MAY–JULY 2021

Morning walk. A chalk-white snail on the path. Agnes Martin. Fox-brown cows against a clump of trees, neon green. The blossom of the blackthorn is as white as sheets on a washing line.

A childhood fantasy: to dissolve into the landscape. Stretch out and turn into earth.

I am closer to others now. But also more lonely.

I wake up thinking about a particular pink colour, sun-bleached on an awning. And against the pink, green shutters and stone. Venice maybe, or Palermo. The smell of rubbish, dogshit, vanilla, tobacco.

> I turn the page in the notebook, and there, in smaller handwriting than the rest, I suddenly see a list of names: Sigrid Karin Sofia and T and Jakob.

I know what she is doing. It's a reminder that we exist, that she is loved.

Is a relationship in fact just a space, you mark the boundaries and walk inside, and there you are. Like a smoking area, outside. Do you just stand there until the cigarette has burnt out?

Sun-drenched piazzas, sleeping dogs, the clutter of crockery, a coffee machine. The sound of shutters opening. The abundance of everyday life. Abundance (someone hoses down the pavement) instead of this melancholy steely thrift.

I dreamt that I could speak to bees. I opened a door to a light corridor, and three bees flew out. I made them fly back in. I opened the next door and hundreds of bees flew out, a dark cloud of them. There were too many – I couldn't reach them or talk to them.

I am running across a piazza at dusk with an old friend from school. We are children and adults at the same time. Laughing, we enter a shop open at night. They sell clothes from HOPE. But also scents. The people behind the counter are young and vibrant. They are drinking prosecco. I open a bottle of scent to test a little on my wrist when I see that it has a big opening, and that the scent is leaking. I quickly turn the bottle and manage to get the cork back in. The perfume evaporates from my hand. 'What amazing reaction time!' the staff call out. 'Well done!'

> I pause at the formulation '. . . when I see that it has a big opening'. It doesn't sound quite right, but then again perhaps the dream is about exactly that: a *big opening* is possible.

> The autocorrect function of my laptop wants to change prosecco to Prozac. We would have laughed at that.

In the next dream I am in Venice. I am finding my way easily. It's so nice to be here. Early morning and there's a breeze from the lagoon, the vaporettos are on the water and the bakeries are opening up . . . I take pictures of everything I see to send to N, but when I look at them I see that there are labels everywhere and I realise that Venice has lost its charm, saturated with commercial interests. Machines, shop windows, products of various kinds . . . But was that not always the case? Have I just never noticed before? Do I feel shame? Does it have anything to do with me, or with us? Are the logos and brands concealing the beauty? But then even the logos are beautiful. Fortnum and Mason, Davidoff . . .

I am wearing shoes with socks. Soon I'll have blisters. I know that. But the pharmacy on Campo San Stefano sells socks. I know that, too.

> That ambivalent knowledge. The beauty, the joy, the ease, but also the shame.

June 3rd, 2021. How could I have believed that the tree was a maple? It's an ash, with long seed pods. When the birds perch on it, it looks like an acacia. If I focus my gaze on the top branches it looks wildly exotic. This tree is for parrots, for hummingbirds, for rare finches. (I wanted to write: for rare thoughts.)

Yesterday I had a glass of wine with my friends S and H. S's laugh is the most amused laugh I know.

It's early in the morning and the city is murmuring. Voices penetrate the murmur. People, birds. Dogs. Now: clearer sounds of cars, the barks of dogs. The murmur is in the background, developing into a hum. But within the hum: the murmur.

The cup of coffee between some books on the windowsill is not steaming, it's smoking. The coffee is smoking a morning cigarette, ice-cool, no guilt. I think it's kind of sexy that we are sharing a flat. The cup is wearing a bone-white one-piece. It doesn't want to be disturbed but it's present in the room, not insensitive to touch, patient. The cup really enjoys life. Now it puts out the cigarette against the window ledge outside and makes itself ready for the day. It's good to have such an inspiring and independent friend. Back turned, it says, 'You know I've always had a weakness for your mouth.' And when I want to respond, only this: 'Enough said, OK?'

Do I have anything to do with the tree? It feels like I do. I have some kind of relationship with it. I think about Morandi's still lifes (again). The spaces in between are so well expressed, shaped and tingly. The spaces in between are not empty.

Friends. Not just to have friends, but to feel that I have friends. They populate me.

I have a glass of wine with J, and A, who has been at a friend's funeral, turns up too. We drink more wine and talk, and whatever we talk about, I don't want it to end, even though we jump between topics, associate, interrupt, insert parentheses into the main thread, parentheses within parentheses. A says that a relationship like his with J is about wanting to be with that person more than with anybody else. 'With a friend, however close we are, in the end I want them to leave. But I never want J to leave.' And when J objects, says that at times he does want to leave, I say, 'But not to go very far.' They have been together for ten years and they look like they have just fallen in love. J says something about the loyalty between them. I think: love, so wonderful but also so dangerous. That feeling of safety which can turn into taking someone for granted. But also, as with them: love as the great curiosity. The safety which means that you can reveal who you are and try and understand it together. The safety which means that time is on your side.

It's almost too much. Well, it is, if you take it all in. Just open your eyes and drink it in. The highest leaves on the top of the tree. Just to see that! I think about coming back to that openness when I'm dying. A drip and a nappy and those top branches. Life on the utmost edge of a possibility. That alone.

Yesterday I longed for Naples. The alleys and Piazza del Plebiscito after the rain. The cobblestones wet and black. The smells released – rubbish (vegetable tops), coffee, burnt sugar, aftershave. Streaks of green smells from the sea, grey from traffic.

Johanna's old friend G comes by, with M.

G's care and tenderness, his love. I thought: it's so beautiful, this person who takes what is good, who knows what he wants. And M so awake and precise. Watchful, testing, and suddenly so obvious in the room, dancing, shining. I just sat and received their love. It should have been enough. But suddenly I missed you. Your hands, just for me. Suddenly it hurt.

The tree is lit up by the sun. The wind sweeps through the leaves. It looks vain, or lazy or impatient. Something in the sight of it doesn't wish me well.

It rained the whole night. The morning is light-grey and still. The tree, the houses, the birds – all is closed and mute. The liveliest sound is a car driving through a puddle. Or is it the movement of the water which sounds alive? And then a drunk man talking loudly in a voice that once said other things. He's wearing a leather hat and a red sports jacket. The voice is insistent, authoritarian.

Behind the grey light a sense of regret, of anguish – grey regret? The song of the blackbird is as crazy as the drunk man's shouts. A thrush, by contrast, is trying to drill a hole in the lid between me and unreality. It's as if some ingredient other than beauty is needed to find one's way to the beautiful.

Something happened. I was walking along Årstaviken when suddenly everything was new, as if I had never seen it before, or never even seen anything like it. I exhaled, an aftershock of fear of being stuck in a narrow, dead way of seeing. A 'no'. A terrifying smallness.

I am at P's house and laburnum and flowers. It's almost 40 degrees. It's early in the morning, the terrace is still cool. I am drinking instant coffee in a green mug with an amusing pattern. There are blue tits nearby, moving about. I didn't know they were so small and tufty, as though they had been washed in hot water and tumble-dried. Yesterday I didn't long for you, or for my child. Everything I needed just then was there. Tomorrow I am picking T up from film camp. We are driving home; she will sit next to me. We'll stop at a petrol station for coffee. Everything will taste good.

P comes out on the terrace, fills my cup with real coffee and asks if I want to dance. Soon, I say.

All the time I spend thinking about you, about us, about the nature of love and the broken soul, about illness, incapacity, and the muteness of speech. Fantasies about us, travel, life, our skin, the colour of your veins . . . It's a liberation when I see you, so I can think about other things.

I exaggerate. I test, experiment. Play. Yes, it is a kind of game. The rules are something of a mirage.

Love is not a room where you go and hang out. Period.

Love is like a luminescence . . . all that . . . the stars, the spectacle, the wonder.

Suddenly everyone seems to be interested in 1. Bird-watching and 2. Zombie films. Are people making themselves older *and* younger at the same time? Is it a way of avoiding the subject? To recognise oneself in flight or quasi-life or both?

Aren't zombies the most ambivalent thing in life?

With my mother at the care home. She is sitting at the table. Coffee and blood stains on the T-shirt which is not hers. I ask how she is. Her hand flutters by her breast. 'Is it the soul, Mum?' I ask. She tries to say something, repeats my word: 'The sun.'

The old dream. I turn to the wall and sink into it. Sink without a trace.

I buy slim cigarettes from the kiosk man. I say: 'I want the slimmest cigarettes you have. I don't really smoke. I just want to look good.' He says: 'You are my wife.' I say: 'I am *like* your wife.' He says: 'She doesn't smoke either.'

I can write with you next to me. The window is open. The heat is tropical. You are lying on the sofa, reading, making notes. Now I stretch out my foot to touch you. The swallows are flying high and there is a fly on the window. They are exactly the same size.

Yesterday morning a moth flew in and fluttered against the walls before resting all day on the base of the ceiling light. By midnight it started fluttering around by the open window. I asked T to turn off the lamp and in the blink of an eye it flew straight out into the illuminated night sky. It made me very happy.

July and there are shades of black in the morning light. The chestnuts with their leaves and branches: a deadly weight. The maple is still (or always) striving upwards. The windows opposite are open. Those who are at home sleep with thin sheets over their bodies, windows open.

For the first time I sense a faint streak of bitterness in my blood. But it's not a streak, it's tiny grains. Is it bitterness? Resentment. I feel resentment. I wrestle with impossibilities.

The blackness sinks to the bottom or is concealed by a blinding sun through the haze. The blackbird pauses. There's only the resonating cooing of the pigeons. The sun looks like a moon behind a washed-out blanket of clouds. Who am I writing this for? Myself. You. You will read this and keep me company. Or keep your distance but still understand. S said yesterday that it's more important to talk about attention than about love.

> Attention. That was something we talked about. The abstract nature of the generic word 'love' as opposed to the granular detail of attention, of listening.

For the first time I notice that the pain frightens me. The sadness of the body. I think you want to, but you can't.

Now it's of great importance to get enough air. Deep breaths.

The grief and the striving.

I long for you. I don't have the energy to long for you.

Freedom from responsibilities. Freedom from action. Freedom – even – from hope?

A salty taste in my mouth when I wake up. Even through the coffee, I sense it. Repressed tears. Hard crystals on my tongue.

Palate/*gommen*. The first word we discussed. We had known each other for maybe an hour.

July 15th, 2021. I cry when I think about our skin. Cry when I think about what we used to call 'point 4'. A point that was empty, inexpressible.

I cried when I thought about the death of our dog Esther and T screaming, beside herself with pain and shock, and the terrifying labour of grief she took on. 'She will never come back!' she screamed.

And about you I think: we will not come back.

I cried when I swam out to the black rocks yesterday morning, the sea as still and smooth as a mirror. It just came to me. I don't know why. Maybe because the sea received me, or because of the beauty, or was it gratitude I felt? Mercy?

S says: 'You do know how little he gives you?' I say, 'I know. I am content with the crumbs. I eat the crumbs.' S says: 'You are not depressive, like me.' I say: 'No, but the last nine months has resembled a depressive state, even though it wasn't. Sadness plus patience probably looks like depression from certain angles. But through all this time I have longed for him, I have felt things, I have reflected. I have been conscious of what is missing.'

I dream that T is playing with TikTok, lying on a narrow iron beam hundreds of metres up in the air. I am there too, and terrified. She lies down on top of me and continues to look at her mobile. How easily we could fall. But she seems entirely safe and unbothered.

I saw an adder on the path along the sea. Half its body was already in the high grass, murky green with a clear zigzag pattern. Was my instinctive response related to the speed of the eye or the speed of the brain? I stopped so fast my feet burnt, but I was not afraid.

That last summer Johanna picked bowls of wild cherries and made pies while I sat outside reading, looking at the sea and the starlings flying in formation over the house.

She was staying with us, but she walked alone early in the morning, mile after mile along the sea.

I walk along the sea, walk to the town, wander around, then come back. I sit on seashells and imagine them as eyelids, each one protecting an eye. The vision, extinguished. Everything fell apart.

Fate. Desolation. A hunger for fate. Fatefulness.

BOOK 9: JULY–SEPTEMBER 2021

I dreamt that T had to flee a diabolical sect in Venice. I whisper that she must run, that we will see each other later. 'Ristorante Madonna four behind San Marco,' I whisper, and she nods and runs through the alleyways towards sharp rocks, precipices, narrow staircases, past donkeys pulling carts, street vendors and beggars. How will she remember the address? How long will she be able to wait once she's there? I run after her. Once I call her name in a crowd of people. Some street dogs are tethered to a high wall on a square. Stately, noble dogs. Somebody has tried to protect them against the sun by fixing up a rug as a makeshift awning. The town is drenched in malice. But there is resistance. Someone points to the barracks. I run towards them, calling T's name in a low voice. She is hiding in a small shed made of plywood; she's in a bath with water up to her nose. It's smart, because if she were to be discovered it doesn't look like she's fleeing. She's just a girl taking a bath.

Later: a dark hall with polished stone floors. My mother in a wheelchair, a Whistler character. She is very concerned with my survival. But that's wrong, she's wrong. The only thing that matters is T.

I dream that someone tells me my handwriting is illegible. And when I write this it almost is illegible.

My godmother has said (and is still saying) some important things: 1. That you can never tell how much of an effort people have made. 2. That we don't understand the first thing about time and ageing. 3. That ending one's life is not as easy as you think, especially if you are very old. 4. To listen to the sighing of the lime trees in the middle of the night, to feel their scent, the breeze passing through branches and leaves into the open bedroom window – to feel the wind touching your skin. Then you don't feel lonely or have the need to feel lonely.

I speak to my brother about Martin Buber and the importance of good luggage. He tells me to read *I and Thou*.

Luggage is about everything . . .

Soon it's the middle of August. The tree outside my corner doesn't say much. It has closed itself up in a combination of fullness and the anticipation of loss. I have to leave it in peace.

Much has to be left in peace.

Something is happening with my vision. Small cascades of golden glitter in the upper field of one eye. And then suddenly a bird (a little tit?), black against the light background of the window ledge. A predator passes by my side. The glitter, the bird and the predator emerge, then cease to exist. They don't go anywhere else. That particular way of ceasing to exist feels very plausible.

I dreamt that I got hold of a sandwich containing ham. It was so foreign to me, the meat (!), a being between slices of bread. Hard to digest – a dead body in the mouth.

> Johanna speculates about the meaning of the dream, but her ideas have nothing to do with her own body. She knows that something is happening with her eye, but she doesn't know what it is. The visual phenomenon is still fascinating to her, not frightening. The dead body in the

mouth makes me think of the tumour behind the eye, a zombie body within the body, but Johanna knows nothing of the cancer as yet.

Everything is metaphor. Even Susan Sontag's book *Illness as Metaphor*, a critique of metaphor in cancer discourse, begins with a metaphor: 'Illness is the night-side of life, a more onerous citizenship. Everyone who is born holds dual citizenship, in the kingdom of the well and in the kingdom of the sick.'

Water must run through the text. Tongues of text right and left. Water courses through in a soft curve, an S-curve, speeding up as it turns. Maybe it's a system, but it mustn't look like it.

I want my thoughts to be like that too, before they end up on paper becoming text. They should stick out, washed clean with running water.

I wake up calm, full and content. A rock, warmed by the sun. There is nothing to worry about. This state of mind is so unusual that I believe, 1. That I am still asleep, 2. That I am suffering from sudden amnesia, and 3. That I will soon understand what is really going on, and see that this state of mind is a particularly effective repressive mechanism. Not even the question of love seems particularly worrying. It's a tight, rough weave with no threads to pull. What kind of a weave? Made by whom?

Don't ask. Don't answer.

How well we engage in the practical, the factual. The labour. Children, how we are, work. Logistics. I search for depth on my own. Loneliness. Longing. And if longing turns into missing, that tone-deaf hunger, then profundity, poetry, the wider views will cease. We'll be in an idiotic place of concrete incomprehension. Things, body, dead ends.

What was the plan?

Ask me anything. I'd like to be given time to reflect, and then answer.

I'd like to think in the world. Eat my way through the world.

The landscape in between the concrete and the abstract. That's where it happens – a wide field of tension. I am talking about a state of mind. Yes. But also about those things pertaining to a packed suitcase, miniature toothpaste tubes and train tickets.

The tree is overripe and tired. Conscious of death,

ravaged. But when the sun shines it comes to life, rearranging itself. The seed pods are like bunches of amber. The leaves, no longer in the best condition, are whispering.

Don't look at me. Listen.

I wish to know whether your love is dissipating. If it's ending, it would be noticeable. But a lessening of love is harder to get the measure of.

I have so many memories of diminishing love or fraudulent love, and how I would compensate with grandiosity and/or new rights – looser reins, lies, a general lack of interest, little loopholes in everyday existence. Leaving on my own with a book (earlier or later, but never at the same time). An obsession with exits.

I and E on Grenada. A small memory, a scene: we are drinking Carib lager. The bottles are wet with condensation. The hotel lobby is brown, there are some dusty palm trees in a pot. Outside the sky is faint lilac, crossed by telephone wires.

We are fine.

My love for him is on the verge of ending.

It's not dramatic, not then, not catastrophic or anguished. There's no need for action. The awful thing, in retrospect, is that he, at that point, knows nothing about it. But also that there is nothing to know. How could I have known that it was the beginning of the end, and not just a new phase of slightly cooler feelings, maybe even a passing phase? It was as though I pushed him aside, creating more space, without (at that point) losing sight of him, or of us.

RuPaul's Drag Race (season 4). One of the 'queens' breaks down when she talks about her childhood and what it was like to be abandoned. She says, 'I'm so tired.' Tiredness. The wish to rest, to be at peace. Care is such a big part of love. To fall asleep without fear, knowing that someone is watching over you.

'I am so tired.'

Unusual rain, small drops falling straight down. The sound is like burning paper. I write my way to meaning and heft. I write to enter into myself.

After nearly a year of quivering (there must be a better word), two internal truths emerge: a greater resistance in me (clearer contours?) and a fearful longing for the world. The fear has to do with metal fatigue . . . The material is brittle rather than elastic. I fear departures, I'm afraid to have to go through yet another hardening process, the vertigo of loneliness and the failure (is there a better word?) to understand the great (possibly imagined) abandonment.

A person with an umbrella passes by on the street below. I see it from above. At the same time the feeling from my dream last night comes back, no images, just a mood. The umbrella is a symmetrical collage of roses, leaves, skyscrapers and crystals. Easy to think of those colours as neon, hard on the eye. But it's as though the rain has washed away the sharpness and the glow. There is something so mild and restful about the spectrum of colours. I don't really have time to properly see it (a skyscraper? a crystal?), but I do have time to think: could this be one of the most beautiful things I have ever seen without really seeing it?

Autumn may be here, not yet visible, but present. The view (the tree, the roofs, the sky) is mute, as though it shrugged its shoulders and turned away. Towards whom? Facing in another direction, it whispers, 'Come and get it.'

No birds. It's as if they never existed. G calls from Öland where the starlings made elliptical shapes in the sky and a sea eagle (G: 'At first I thought it was a person') sat on a rock by the sea during our conversation. What extravagance. Here my tab of the world offers the least possible revelation – it's mean as hell.

I go back to my book. Suddenly something happens. I read a page, look up, and the view has changed, subtly. I do it again: read a page, then look up. Yes, it has changed. Something about the tone of colour, the expression. The next time I do it the roof is about to take off like a black crow or a knife. The tree says: 'There are others like me in another part of the world.'

And the sky? What does it say? Could it be an expression of fanatical indifference? The people in Kabul fell through it from the wings of the airplane. The screams from Haiti dispersed in it, and the smoke from the fires. The sky tells us that everything will be fine but it doesn't mean anything by it. (And the sound of shooting from Tensta during the night.)

In a dream I hear a voice say: 'In the midst of raging war, someone put an ice cube in her glass.' The image becomes a scene in books, on film. A café in Beirut, Paris, Tel Aviv. A glass of soda water, Campari? What era are we in? What war? Who is she? I don't see her. Who put the ice in her glass?

Outside the window it's snowing. No, it's bright little insects moving back and forth. It's one of the last days of August. I want to say something between the lines, behind them. There is an ache behind the words. Of course it's not snowing. And yet it is. Time seems to stand still since you got ill a year or so ago. Later it often snowed outside my window. An after-construction: that the snowflakes, too, were particles of a catastrophe. A silent explosion. The reminder of a breakdown.

To sit alone in a chair, reading. (The August night is so dense that the black roof opposite is invisible. The window is a mirror. The ceiling light is a full moon and the bookcase casts a twin image on the façade opposite. The act of describing makes me less lonely. I don't know if there is hope in the text. But in writing there is always hope.)

To sit alone in an armchair surrounded by love. Or to be without love, without the feeling of love, the assurance of love, its warm wind and abundance. What does it do to me, to always have to start again, ask myself the question, reassure myself, tell the story of us?

It gnaws at me, the tiredness. It gnaws at me, my docility which is beginning to imitate indifference, sleep and grief. Yet another loneliness within the loneliness.

Sometimes I think that you will get well and fall in love with a young, introverted woman from a distant place (distant from my point of view). And I will become older than my years, robustly swimming towards myself, that is to say, towards land.

And you will not love me.

Nor I you.

I write my way from nothingness. Or am I writing my way towards it? Am I writing an ending? An ending that will heal us? Are the words too big? But weren't we going to be big?

A bit of the night still hangs in the tree like the after-image of a face, an oval shape. Timing. Someone in hiding steps forwards or, unnoticed, finds another hiding place. The night seems to be sucked up by the tree trunk and the branches. A similar pain. And inside there are transport routes and systems, possibilities to spread out and be transformed into a breath.

Here follows a dialogue, I think with Johanna's psychoanalyst, H:

'When have you been happiest during this last year.'

'I have been happiest in my hopes about love.'

'And the best moments.'

'In the dark, in my bed, when we were able to speak very intimately.'

'And that sense of closeness, were you able to recreate it in other situation and environments.'

'No, that's hard. I think we rationalise it. We work and take care of our children. I don't know what's happening inside him.'

'What are you thinking about.'

'His heavy hands. And about how I want to see him. I would wish us to be warm. I don't know . . .'

'What is it you don't know.'

'I don't know.'

'It hasn't been a bad year, but it has been a difficult year. What happens to one's sense of longing, in the end? Where does it go? What traces does it leave?

Yesterday: my mother. I held her gaze until she could say my name. With my eyes I called forth her voice, my name.

All that gold, that stuff glittering in the corner of my eye. What does it say about me that I thought about it as beautiful rather than as a sign that there is something wrong with my vision?

The clouds are like ships in the sky. They are really going somewhere. This way! Once there, they sink down to the quay and fold up, turning into paper planes or miniature notebooks. There's the next Armada, and the next one.

I remember London, the flights from Heathrow, how I could count the seconds between the planes in the sky. An exact rhythm.

My fear of death is about being abandoned. To be abandoned by life.

Life, death, light, shadows. Yesterday I went to a poetry reading. I had a glass of wine and then I cried. A flood of tears which started between the words, during a pause of no more than a second.

Now it's morning. Below the window there's a long line of people for the bakery. There's some movement in the tree, behind a waterfall. I can't see through my right eye, or at least what I see is very blurry. My face is dark and contour-less in the bathroom mirror, as though an internal light had been switched off.

The wind through the window smells of water. Melting snow. The wind comes from far away. There's a pale cloud-cover over the sky. An airplane flies in the opposite direction. Opposite, because the fine-grained pattern in the sky faces the other way.

It's raining gold through my eye.

Sunday.

I close my eyes. My feet are on the warm radiator. I feel the morning chill against my cheek and throat. Coffee. The bark of a dog. Such an incredible silence in the middle of the city.

September 1st, 2021. Johanna finally sees the optician for her eye. He tells her to take a taxi straight to hospital. But Johanna – a gesture, a life hack – goes to NK first to buy scent.

She texts me from the hospital. I ask how she is. 'It's like trying to see through Vaseline,' she responds.

The mass in my eye. That's what it's called. Mass, in anticipation of another word. All the golden powder shimmering and falling through the corner of my eye. A heap of gold. Like the finest salt, sugar or sand. A golden cushion in my eye. My poor eye. I try to look at the sick eye in the bathroom mirror. Does it look tired? Sad? It doesn't glitter. The brain has abandoned it, focusing on the eye that's well. My sick eye is just an image of an eye.

Golden stuff – hourglass – time. Signs one doesn't understand, can't interpret. Golden stuff, glitter, lightning – my eye is sick. My eye.

I want to be near the people whose doors I don't have to knock on.

At the window early mornings, I often think about how I need onions. Or that I'm running out of cinnamon. Sunflower seeds. Yeast. Dishwasher tablets, coffee filters. Not all of it, but one or two things. I think about the food in the cupboard and in the space above the cupboard, so that I will never need anything.

Today is a perfect day for a visit to the oncology ward. To the oncologist. To see an oncologist. The word is unfathomable. Round and cool, light blue. It's a mythical being. On the one hand. On the other: I might have a tumour in my eye. It's September.

Johanna wrote to me after the tests:

'S, I'll call later. But it's not good news. The only important thing now is that it hasn't spread to the liver or lungs. The eye will be irradiated within 3 weeks. It's absolutely possible that everything will be fine after that. But I will lose 90 per cent of my vision in that eye. Xxxxx'

I read the text and felt a wave of faintness. Someone got me a chair and a glass of water.

I have never been able to imagine the future. I could never quite go there, maybe because I'm so preoccupied with reality, and reality is primarily now. It's as if memories (not just mine – all memories) are true but only last for the second you remember. Is that strange?

I have given T breakfast in bed. She is so quiet on her mobile. The air feels autumnal. The window is closed. My stomach is gurgling. I am hungry as a wolf.

The man who interviewed me for the nice literary podcast asks, 'Can you imagine a life without writing?

If anything should happen to you . . . ? The thought that what happened to your mother could happen to you, too . . . ?' I answer that I can't imagine it. But that I think I might have a good life without writing anyway.

After he left, I realised that I can't imagine a life at all. Is that even possible? Isn't life itself the one thing you can't imagine? Isn't it just as impossible to imagine life as it is to imagine death?

It isn't impossible to imagine death.

It's much simpler than all that stuff – life – I didn't imagine.

When I close my eyes to fall asleep, a light moves around under the right eyelid. It reminds me of something. A moon crescent, a blinding shard of light. Where have I seen it before? In a documentary about space? It occurs to me that the eye receives, it does not transmit. Well, the gaze transmits, but it's always an answer. The eye answers. Lying in the dark I realise that whatever is happening behind my eyelid, behind the eye, is a phenomenon.

Is it the passing headlights of a car on a black rainy night? Not quite. A solar eclipse? Maybe.

Apart from having a child this is the biggest thing I have ever done in my life: to love someone, and then to wait for him to get better. Then to fall ill myself, and to appreciate life.

This thing about 'starting again'. This thing about 'finding one's way back'. To reinterpret experiences, or just live with them. I baked scones. London weather, a light fog. The smell of coffee lingers like thought bubbles over the cups. I am very tired of the mood of partings. Of endings, weighing us down. A silence suddenly, the awareness that something is not being said.

You say that the place in you which previously was black with guilt and anguish is now white and blank. An empty space, waiting to be filled. You make sense, and you are credible. Two good things.

Someone leaves. Perhaps he'll come back. On a day like this, do I even have the energy to guess?

For a terrible moment I think my tree has fallen. I can't see one side of the crown and imagine it broken, fallen against the building. My tree is a person who is ill or very exhausted, leaning against a wall. The tree closes its eyes and inside the eyelids it sees nothing. And that is a relief.

Have I left you? By returning to that room again. The unfurnished one, a space of darkness. Still as a pond. A widening pupil of blackness. That place has no words and nor does it give words. When you arrive, you can take a deep breath. I know now that the place exists. That is a relief.

I remember a picture book with pages sometimes halved or shared. One landscape became two. An interior became an exterior. Kelly, Dot and Esmeralda stepped through a painting and suddenly they were in the landscape of the image. And in Sendak's *Where the Wild Things Are* the walls became the world all around.

The walls, my walls. The words. The eyes.

Love.

A mole on the bottom of the eye.

The mole on the bottom of the eye may have been there since the beginning. Exactly like this text. Degrees of life and mortal danger.

I open Johanna's poetry collection, *Rachels hus*, and find a poem that seems to speak through time:

I wake up in my bed and remember
all the other beds I once slept in.
Beds I woke up in.
Their place in the room.
The direction and the height.
A thousand directions.
Directions now crossing.
And I get up and fumble
for doors in the air.
Seeking handles, hinges.
I get up and fall
when I step into something
which no longer exists.
I walk into walls
that I think are rooms,
fall over thresholds I can't fathom.

Who sees me in this bloody
      blind man's buff?
Sees me hurt myself on my past.
How dream-like memories return,
catch me up and turn me
round and round.
And those I didn't think could speak,
they are not speaking.
But the walls can see me now
that I am blind.

Johanna Ekström, *Rachels hus*,
tr. Sigrid Rausing

BOOK 10: SEPTEMBER–OCTOBER 2021

I don't know what kind of a morning it is, I can't tell what I see any more. The tree is underwater blurry. I float on my back just under the surface of the water looking up at real life.

I pretend that the wind makes the house flutter and tremble and that the tree stands absolutely still, sensitive to another kind of wind, another frequency.

The wasps are the same colour as the seed pods of the maple. They fly in through the window, circle the room, then fly out again. They always find their way out. I just closed the window and they come and knock on the windowpane. I wonder what they want. Once in, they don't take anything. Is it just entry they want? This thing: to be allowed in.

For the first time ever, I'm afraid of the dark, sensitive to unexpected noise and movements, the shadows from the candles flickering on the windowsill. My tired eye misjudges distance, making the world at the same time double and flat. My pen doesn't reach the paper. My wine glass hits the sofa table, hard. I sense a presence.

I am frightened but I make my fear smaller until it turns into feeling spooked by the dark.

I feel like someone is watching me. I want to be seen, of course, but without fear.

The worst thing about being afraid of the dark is that it's not me. I am not afraid of the dark. I have become someone else. Is the frightening image I can see from the corner of my eye in fact me?

I dream about a creaking sound behind my back. A mouse? The wall is made of beadboard. By the base, a little pile of sawdust. The wall is so thin. Now it trembles. A gap opens up and I see a tool, a steel rod with a little scoop made of grey rubber. 'Hello!' I call. I glimpse my neighbour's flat through the gap. She's moving in there. 'Hi!' she calls back, adding something to do with the wall. Suddenly she's in my flat, talking, her face blotchy and red, upset. I don't understand where I'm living and why the walls have become so unreliable.

I am worried that my friends won't trust me any more because I am ill and soon I'll only see out of one eye.

I am not being careless, but I make mistakes. Say it, say it again. Do it, do it again. My new sentence: 'I don't know.' It feels wrong, even though it's true.

Yesterday I tidied the shelves above the kitchen counter. There was a butterfly in a glass frame. I took it down and looked at the little point of glue between the glass and the abdomen of the butterfly. I let it slide into the bin. But perhaps it was not a real butterfly? Was it a miniature paper dragon?

If night is coming soon, it might as well come now. The first act of dusk. Outside the window everything is made of paper, cut pieces badly glued together. There is no light in the light but nor is there any darkness in the grey. In my eye: a thirst.

My dreams last night were salty with tears. Fragments: I am feeding a child. People whose faces I don't recognise are coming towards me from all directions. I don't know if they are circling me or walking past me.

Even in the mornings I feel spooked. The sound of the lift, a door opening, footsteps in the stairwell or in the flat above. It's as though I always (consciously) have been prepared. Born prepared for an intrusion or a parting. Ready to handle it, to stand up and smile, to protect myself and take responsibility for whoever is coming towards me or leaving.

The wind makes the crown of the tree sway as if it were underwater, moving in the currents on the bottom of the sea. I wonder: what is the difference? Is there any difference?

The light is dull and dying. My interest in the movements of the tree borders on anxiety. I hear a machine droning, the hum of children's voices. I don't hear the tree.

Evening. I am trying to light the candle in the window. I think there must be something wrong with the wick, then I realise that I am holding the match in the air behind it.

It's so real, but it's a dream. On the floor: a silver chain, very fine. I bend to pick it up. Then it starts moving, crawling like a centipede across the floor towards the wall. I try to hold it, but it slips under my fingers. I press it down with my nail, crying out for help. Someone has to investigate, and name it. I know it's dangerous and I know it's getting away. It came out of my body. I cry out one more time, lose my grip and it slides into the gap between the floor and the wall.

I remember other dreams about things, half-beings or people disappearing between floors and walls, sinking into the earth or falling into walls and vanishing. When I was a child electricity cords would coil up and come to life. A baby dug a hole in the ground between some paving stones and pressed its downy head against the earth and disappeared. My brother's legs stuck out from under the sofa and he asked who would love him when my parents were done loving him. A black dog ran towards me and vanished in my body. But the fine silver chain in the dream was harmful. Blind, steered by will alone. I have a fine gold chain round my neck. I took it off during the ultrasound. The radiologist helped me to put it back on. Silver . . . silverfish. Those beings that glide over floors, roll into balls, extend into chains, disappear into cracks. Would you call them vermin? The word makes me think of dust and crumbs, hair and nails. Not damage. But they are a sign. Like the silver chain in my dream. Something is wrong. I am ill.

Say it: I am ill.

A cloud bank and in front of it: the tree, lit up by the afternoon sun. The tree is a whole forest. Rousseau, a black panther, a naked woman on a divan. The greenery is as shrill as the laughter from the house opposite. The leaves are sketched in sharp shadows against the branches. An airplane crosses the boundary between clear-blue sky and dark clouds. A stub of a pencil is about to say something of decisive importance.

My friends:

P has had the boys over the weekend and now suddenly feels lonely in the large house. Dusty floors. A melancholy so sharp it cuts her. Spaghetti and Netflix with the cat and the dog. But also: a lover, a lot of laughter, and – recently – long car rides in the middle of the night.

J feels anxious about a mammography result and flees to the country. She swims in the sea. Two women pass her by. Why don't they stop, say hello, or at least ask about the temperature of the water?

C is writing an article and is playing with the idea of becoming a transvestite.

K is travelling across Judea.

I dream about a large sheet of paper with text. I am lying down with my cheek against it, trying to decipher the text. I say: 'I can't see sideways any more.'

> According to the notebooks, someone calls from the hospital at this point, telling Johanna that 'everything will be fine': the ultrasound of the liver and other organs shows no metastases. She already knew – the radiologist, warm and communicative, had told her at once. She stood on the street outside, called me, and cried with relief.
>
> The hospital confirmed: the result (negative) of the ultrasound was '100 per cent true'.

The seagulls fly in pairs and so do the pigeons, their movements so finely calibrated and close. Then I understand that I am seeing double.

I dream about an open place. Sunset, sand and sharp grass under my feet. An empty plastic bottle is rolling in the wind. I am free to go anywhere. But as soon as I start moving the ground under my feet turns into wet soil, heather, moss, entangled roots. A resistance arises. It's almost impossible to get out. I give up. Then the open landscape returns, the landscape without resistance.

A memory from my first visit to the eye oncology ward. All the rooms are new, uninhabited, the building itself is new. There is no lingering atmosphere in the corridor. Pale colours and here and there a bright-red piece of furniture or an orange artwork. Red means blood. How could it mean anything else, here?

The façade opposite is new, too. I see no one through the windows. The only living thing is a species of ornamental grass trembling in the wind. A father and daughter pass by my waiting room. The daughter jumps and skips, throwing her hair back. I have time to think that she must have accompanied her father to his appointment when I realise the opposite must be true, and veer away from the thought.

The leaves of the chestnut tree are turning yellow. My cinnamon tree seems unbothered. Late to come into leaf, it is also late to lose its leaves. I have long since lost interest in the tree opposite.

The concept: to step out of time. To dream by the window – is that to step out of time? Or is it the opposite – to step into time?

Memories of the dance floor. N dancing. Liljeholm bridge. It was a summer night. Were we teenagers? What were we?

Nightmares, fragments from horror movies. I am anaesthetised with an injection and beaten, I try to scream and can't. Meaningless violence. After such a night: I open the window. It's damp and mild out-side, the sky is baby-blue. The world looks stable. The houses with their invisible foundations. The trees with their roots. The pigeon balancing on the gutter. The seagulls flying over the roofs, morning sun under their wings.

I wrote to you last night. I couldn't take it any more. I was upset, like a child. A child? Yes, in the sense that my feelings were very acute. Waiting was not possible. A child needs comfort now. Everything else is too late. I wrote to you but sent it to myself. Today, seeing the message and the information 'read yesterday', I trick myself into believing that you read it. The information – *read yesterday* – is so intimate and tender.

A bird flies past the window in its airspace. As far as I could see it was as soft as a dachshund puppy. Not a thing with feathers, hope and grief.

Someone I know sends me a text and I am floored by her image of me as seriously ill. What does 'seriously' mean? And what is serious? Death is serious and so is long-term pain, long suffering. I think of myself as having a difficult condition rather than a serious one. Life is serious. My eye (a part of me) has a serious illness. What does serious mean? It's something that will take time and energy to solve, to digest, to crack.

I had imagined the love between me and N as easy *and* serious, not difficult. But I was wrong. It was easy to love, but the love was very difficult.

Is this comprehensible?

Does it have to be?

C says that he is impressed by my resolution and strength. But: 'I am not saying that's necessarily a good thing. I mean, I'm impressed. But that's not a compliment.'

A dream: on the roof opposite a very small person is climbing. A grown man in a black hoodie. He is carrying something. I photograph him with my phone.

He disappears. I look up. He's standing on the window ledge outside, holding on to the roof. He has no face under the hood: it's a black hole. Under each arm a bunch of birchwood. Or is there something wrong with the dimensions? I can't see. Could those be hot dog buns under his arms? Where is he from? I know that, at least. The Planet of Screams. Is that where I am? Someone's banging loudly, impatiently, on my door. They want to get in. Have to get in. I wake up. The banging carries on, harder, faster. I wake up.

> I think about Johanna's previous dream about ham, flesh in the mouth, and a faceless tumour spreading like fire through her body. Something wants to come in.
>
> And what about the repeated phenomenon about seemingly waking up from a dream, when she is still dreaming. The borderline between dream and reality feels very thin.

A long centipede is crawling on the floor of an empty white room. It's black, with some minor yellow spots. I want to get it out of the room. I don't want to kill it and I don't want it to disappear in a crack in the floor and come back later. I spray water on it and it curls up. I spray it again and it uncoils, moving across the floor with unexpected speed. It crawls over the threshold into another empty room. By the far wall are small piles of sawdust and tiny gnawed holes in the skirting board. The centipede crawls towards a hole and disappears. The rooms are empty, tarnished, unsafe.

I am not sitting in my chair. I don't want to see the tree. Because I can't see it clearly, I avoid it. Instead, I sit on the sofa facing the bookcase and see only walls and roofs through the window. A pigeon. An insidious and at the same time tangible feeling comes to me: that my blurry vision is connected to the rest of my body, even though the problem is only in my eye. Everything feels proximate. The uncertainty in the body and everything around it. 'And the walls became the world all around.' I don't want this openness, this permeability. It's not freedom, it's insanity. Not a safe place.

The wall is transforming.

The walls that are the world. Is it strange that it frightens me?

I take the rubbish out. The bins are in the storeroom round the corner. As I come out of the room I stand for a while by the door, which I have shut behind me. It's a space neither alien nor at home.

I don't see double but whatever I see is bent and proximate, more a suggested reality, a sketch, than reality itself. And the experience of that seems to spread to all my other senses – hearing and feeling. It's as though I have been drugged. I don't understand the world.

Correct that. I have to correct it: I don't understand the world *around me*. Does that make it better? More local. Like the tumour in my eye – a local tumour. Only there.

When I saw . . . That walk, the children who threw a water balloon on the pavement where we walked. I jumped, then carried on talking. But N was frightened, as though we'd been in an accident. And of course, in a sense he was right – for him it was serious. He lingered, wanted to find out where the balloon had been dropped from. He stayed with the experience for a long time, and right then our life together somehow turned rigid and bare. Humourless. Skin and bones. Streets black with rain. I could have ended it then. I could have said, this is not who I am. There's not enough of me in this. *This is too alienating.* But I was afraid of becoming a stranger myself, afraid of embodying alienation, so I said nothing. I wanted everything to be easy again. For our conversation to find its tone, its flow of subtext and associations.

> I think of Johanna's memory of the liquorice lolly at Skansen. Her terror that something alien would invade her body. The fear of becoming someone else. A child of others. The fear that she herself would turn into a stranger.

I dream that someone says, 'The independence nut has to be cracked.' But what does it mean? Cracked is a terrible word. To crack up, to be broken, to be hurt. Is it about the tumour? My eye, which is going to be opened. The tumour, which will be cracked? And the frightening, faceless little man in my dream a week ago – was he the tumour, too? Face like a black hole because it's missing, or because I can't see it? It's as though the faceless black hole was my pupil, too.

Next to me on the bedside table there's a small notebook and pencil. I have made some notes in the middle of the night. 'Keep to the essence!', 'Keep to the subject!'. The dreams come back. They are painful but they don't wish me ill. The person speaking in my dream, how can she be me and not-me at the same time?

I am standing with a man – we are in a relationship – behind some tall, dirty-blue buildings. Powder snow on last year's leaves and frozen grass. Traces of our footsteps in frost and mud. He is shouting at me, telling me off. I haven't done anything. My face feels alien. He looks at me and thinks he has me all figured out. In his hatred there is relief. I'm not of any use to him. It's about his friend R, whom I have treated badly. I admit that R and I are not close. But I like her, I am curious about her. 'Don't try it on! You are so arrogant! You are just acting. Your behaviour is unforgivable!'

'But I am really not the kind of person who pours a glass of wine or makes coffee and offers biscuits while smiling falsely. I don't do things like that. It's true that I find her a bit difficult. But not that difficult. I would have said if I didn't want her to come. I would have told you.'

He doesn't believe me. Maybe he doesn't hear me. Maybe he doesn't want to believe me or hear me. I am shouting now, beside myself: 'But what shall I do? Say it! Say what you want me to do!'

He gives me a distant look, answers: 'Talk in

sequences. Talk in sequences and keep to the essence, the subject.'

I am standing by some university buildings, the same dirty-blue façades as in the last dream. But now I am at the front of the buildings, facing Stora Skuggan a kilometre or so away across the fields. It looks different from when I was a child. At that time there was only one narrow road, curving round the fields. After the first bend one could catch a glimpse of our house. Now there are three roads, two of them new, tarmac glistening black, and the old one. The fields are broken up. Between the three roads: mud and diggers, deep holes, fallen trees and massed roots. Some drug addicts are sitting on one of the fallen trees. On the ground: syringes and empty plastic bottles.

Someone is sleeping under a digger. I can choose any one of the three roads to get home. And even though I have to pass by the people who are so broken and sick I take the old road, the one I am familiar with. I walk over roots across frozen mud, over planks of wood and reinforced iron bars thrown haphazardly on the ground.

In front of me I see a being crawling on all fours. He is very ill. No teeth, skin covered in sores. He is like the ground on which I walk. He vomits and a liquid teeming with larvae, barely visible, comes out of him. And I know that the larvae have contaminated me, or that I will become contaminated. Yes, they are in my blood, and I can see with my inner eye how they are moving towards my heart, my liver, my kidneys. I must get home. If I get there in time I will not die.

The viral larvae are on their way to my heart. I am on my way home. It's a life-and-death struggle.

Can I take a plane from here? Suddenly I'm at an airport. I seem to be first in line for the next flight. But an air stewardess in a wrinkled red apron informs me that the queue is in alphabetical order. Like this, she says, moving her hand over some books on a shelf.

My body is transparent. I am a computer screen, a computer game. The viral larvae move in rows, shiny white against dark-red veins. I explain that I have to get home, that I must get there soon. The air stewardess asks, 'But what is the central point here? Explain the central point, the essence!'

The stretch of land which separates me from home is now entirely covered by roots, a network of vessels identical to that which I sometimes see when I close my sick eye.

The unconscious, that shadowy self beyond the self which we think about in symbolic and abstract terms, urges Johanna time and time again to keep to the subject. The essence – I imagine – is the tumour. But how to avoid confusing her illness with older layers of existential pain – roots, home, childhood? How to avoid creating metaphors of it, connections between a series of losses – the loss of a sense of safety, of her lover, of sight, perhaps of life itself? How to avoid mixing up the metaphorical seeing and blindness with actual seeing and blindness? How do you keep two world views, the one of biology, the other of the mind, apart?

Cancer cells are random; the world of the body a biological and evolutionary machinery without mercy or ethics. The cells float in the blood and lymphatic system on the long journey towards heart, liver, kidneys. Is there communication between them, are there microscopic threads of cancer between the organs or do the cells travel one by one like aimless meteors in space?

I don't know. But I am thinking again

about Johanna's reflections on despair, the 'shining net of blackness':

'The body is black and inside it the organs hang close together, isolated in their own nets, their own languages. They are luminous like planets. It's beautiful but there's no point trying to understand it.'

Dancing Gaga with N at the Ballet Academy. The joy of it! An abundance of happiness. Inexpressible. That he said yes straight away, and entered into it so experimentally, so openly. It was my thing but also so obviously his. He understood it. My embarrassment and shyness and pride. We were independent, and there was such happiness in that slightly performative (on my part) independence. A performance without pain. We looked at each other across the floor of the great hall and after the last dance we ran up to each other and hugged and our bodies were so obvious through our clothes. As though we were naked. Which, of course, in a way we were.

You will disappear.

You disappear. You are walking backwards out of the picture. Something is erased, becomes inexpressible, is forgotten. That, too, is a dance. We could have laughed at that dance. But we are not laughing. What I remember is already so long ago. A thousand years ago. Your skin, our skin . . . the taste in our mouths.

When the torment of the soul ceases, the questions of the soul cease too. That is the effect of antidepressants. We become deaf to the soul.

I see the jay! My tree has lost a third of its leaves, and at the very top is the jay. I dream that it picks my tumour out with its beak, straight through the pupil. The tumour is a little nugget of gold.

   No, I didn't dream it. I made it up.

You brought me to a birthday party with relatives. The party didn't represent 'you'. I wanted you to come to a family dinner. The dinner wasn't 'me'. But the recognition, the ability to interpret and fit into the dinner, was mine. So in that way it represented a part of my origins. And the same for you, even if both events were exaggerated caricatures, especially when we compared them. Which I think we did, but we didn't compare *us*. Not in such general terms. Not in terms of value, strength, aesthetics. But we did talk about class. Often.

The leaves on the tree are more sparse and shrunken now. In the dull light, the unlight, I could have imagined that the tree had been exposed to severe drought, that the crown could rattle. But these are redundant speculations – it's raining, and the streets are wet.

The day of the operation. I can have clear liquids for another hour. I want to be precise in my speculation about the tree. But nothing I write is really true, or relevant or interesting. Only this: that the tree looks like two trees, one that is well and one that is sick. Two states of ageing. Or: two methods for survival.

T gets dressed. She is humming. I have a moon crescent in my eye which comes and goes. A planetarium. The valved projection of space. I wonder: how much light enters into my brain if the right eye can't see?

Where is the rage? No, I meant, where is *my* rage? That's what I should write. Formulate the right question. It hits internally, the after-tremors visible from the outside. Because I failed in understanding and forgiveness? I want to get away from those words.

Before I lock the door to go to the hospital I bend down to pick up a grain of pearl sugar in a corner. I catch it with the tip of my finger and let it out through the window.

Note the tender formulation. The sugar, a grain, is caught and *let out*. It is freed, not thrown out. It has a certain kind of life. Like the pillowcase, tucked round the radiator. Like having eye contact with snowflakes. Johanna perceived life in her room, semi-beings with feelings and thoughts. Like a prisoner in an isolation cell, she observes light, balls of dust, insects.

At the hospital she is anaesthetised, and the surgeon places a thin radioactive shield near the tumour and what is called the macula, the yellow spot on the retina at the back of the eye where the rods and the cones, the light-sensitive cells evolved for seeing, are most dense. The tumour will be irradiated. During that time – a few days in hospital – Johanna herself becomes radioactive, and visitors have to sit on her right side, since the radiation is directed towards the left.

When the treatment was over, she was anaesthetised again, the shield was removed, and she was released from hospital. The eye was very swollen and red.

We still thought it was just about the eye.

When night comes and dark fills the large hospital window in my room, my courage runs out. It's all gone. I get paracetamol and a sandwich. I pull off the crusts so only the soft bread remains.

I remember how we laughed at the starlings eating all the sour cherries and messing up your car. I remember how red the cherries were, as though they were lit up from the inside. The summer before last. Our happy summer.

(But didn't I already know? Yes, I knew.)

We made such a big thing out of those birds. We told the story over and over and everyone found it funny. We laughed and kissed. There was something so triumphant and generous about letting a laugh turn into a kiss.

Now I am thinking about the fall from those heights. But that may not be right. I mean something different.

There was a lack, somehow, of other stories, of smaller, more private words creating a base. A weave, between us. Maybe you didn't have the energy, maybe you didn't know how, or didn't want to. Maybe you missed some indefinable thing in me. Did you feel my longing, and did you evade me even then?

Here, in hospital, you are almost disappearing, even as a face. It's so quiet. Just the clock ticking. Soon I will take a shower. The nurse will change my sheets, check my blood pressure and give me eye drops.

The thought of our story empties me of meaning, like the books I brought with me, which seem meaningless now. Whatever I read disappears line by line, as though my eye is not reading but erasing. That's probably neither strange nor mysterious. But my perception of reality is weak and maybe I have always known that it would abate, lighten, get absorbed in other things – and that it is precisely for that reason that I have struggled so hard to show that I exist.

Home. Trying to understand the pain I think about giving birth. Most women who have given birth can relate to that. But to give birth was also a joy. I remember the curiosity between the contractions and the knowledge that something good would come of it.

When the pain ceases, I feel gratitude, then amnesia, then fatigue. At that point, having forgotten the pain, I don't know why I am so tired. And yet I think: I have no margins left. If even the smallest thing were to happen now that would cause me pain I would feel despair.

Despair. What does it mean?

I'm at home. J picked me up. For now, he's my older brother. He tells me that last night, as he was making dinner, he suddenly felt a stabbing pain in his right eye. He has tears in his eyes as he tells me this.

Not to be allowed to be ill. Not just *to do* the wrong thing, but also (worse) to *be* wrong.

Memories of childhood. Memories of the trip to Cuba. Memories (S reminds me) of anorexia. It's as if the illness is a reprimand. An accusation I have to turn away from.

S reminds me.

I remember it.

The pain washes over me and far away, by the outer perimeter of thinking, the tears get ready. But I don't want to cry – I'm scared that the tears will hurt my eye even more. I have to follow the pain, not resist it. In resistance, the impossible is born.

I remember leaving T at nursery, how she took care of the separation, how we shared it.

Later: the divorce, when she was five.

Later: how she hesitated about a sleepover with a friend, digested her preconceptions and anxiety and finally went off as though it were nothing.

As if the resistance, the refusal, the impending panic would burn the pain to the body, scarring it. Something permanent.

I remember my own panic as a child. How I would abandon myself to a state of hysteria. Did I do it in order to be believed, or in order to cease to exist? I responded to feeling irrelevant by becoming or experiencing myself as crazy. A no worse than a no. I was zero.

The ego (present, palpable) says *yes* inside its no. But to become nothing, to become zero, is to lose one's sense of self.

It's very windy. I go out and feel dizzy and helpless. The tree has lost most of its leaves. The backs of the leaves are silvery pale. They have no resistance, bend to the wind as they wouldn't have done this summer. Disappearances are frightening. It is, if not deliberate, the consequence of something else. The consequence of a disappearance is frightening.

The action in the disappearance is frightening.

A fly, the shadow of a fly. Then it takes off, flies out of the window, gathering height like a signature tune without a melody.

I bend over to pick up a dustball. But I am touching a shadow. My fingertips against the blank surface of the floor.

I have to remember the nights a year or so ago. Your first disappearance. I would wake up crying like a child. As I came to from the anaesthetic I experienced something similar, but without grief. The feeling of surfacing from an inexpressible darkness. Disembodied spirit. My body was neither dressed nor undressed. It was as if life was only about temperature. The presence of warmth.

My beloved. I was not meant to be with you. I will remember you and forget. It will be fine.

I seem to seriously believe that I am sitting here making my way into the world. In any case I know with certainty that the world has made its way into me. I am changing. I keep some things, leave others behind. The sky is clear. The leaves turned from me, a gesture of rejection. Now they turn again, but the indifference remains.

I have painted my nails red. It looks good. I write this instead of writing something else to remind myself that I am a woman. Not a man. Not dead.

Evening. My left eye is tired now. The right one is at a standstill. Nebulas of pulsating contours. Field of visual noise. I'm alone here.

I think I'm writing a fragment of a longer story. There is no other way, there is only writing.

BOOK 11: OCTOBER–NOVEMBER 2021

October 20th, 2021. Yesterday I poured wine outside my glass and put my hand in the flame of a candle. Today it's easier to walk. But on streets I don't know I feel uncertainty, not curiosity. Every now and then I put my feet down like an old person or an addict. I am afraid of electric bikes, lamp posts, and sometimes the walls of buildings.

The tree is bare now. But something is still there. Seed capsules? Pendants?

I feel the sadness in my arms. A low hum. Also in my breasts and mouth.

In my dream: a man with a shapeless black dog on a lead, near a tree. He warns me, says the dog is having a bad day and is not reliable. 'Keep your distance,' he says. I try to see if I can get in between the dog and the tree, or if I have to walk round. The nearer I get to the tree, the more difficult it is to move. It's like wading through water. Suddenly my face is pressed up against it. I believe my legs are strong, but I seem to be lacking some muscle and I can't move sideways. I have to get round the tree to my left. The black dog is panting on my right.

A night without nightmares. That feeling of my own thin skin, my vulnerability, is a little less acute. I have added the word *acute*.

My right pupil almost covers the whole iris. It's a dark eye now.

The distance. That word in the dreams. The act. Distant but present? I know I am writing about my own longing rather than about you. I am trying to express you, to convince me. Distance you, and come closer to myself.

To have great hope (or, worse, expectations), to be disappointed and abandoned. To stand, hands open and empty. To stand naked, waiting . . . I learnt early on how ugly that was. As though one should walk through the world radiating strength and desire.

Also, this thing about being ill: the lack, the weakness of the physical construction. The mistake. The impossibility.

Everyone tells me I'm strong. I know. You have to be strong to admit your weakness. Strong enough to write it. Strong enough to laugh at it. Or at something else.

My uncertain vision is spreading to my memory. A blurry image somehow speaks to forgetfulness. The more I try (and fail) to see, the more memory I lose. What is it like? What does it remind me of? I don't know because I can't remember, can't reach clarity. If it's not in front of me, it must be in my past. But when I turn round there's nothing there.

I try to find sustenance in memories of us, but they are far away, concealed behind all the stillness, waiting, immobility. In that stillness there were some moments of tenderness, sudden intimacy, laughter, a little sex. Conversations about words and books. A few conversations about us. A few attempts to get clarification or even to create a coherent image of you.

But it's not you I am grieving for now.

I have to stretch out, take hold of people to really see them. And to really see myself. That's my task now.

The uncertainty: that I don't know what others see when they look at me. It's as if my own faulty vision is a fault line in me. As if my blurry vision makes me blurry, too.

Anorexia was the ideal illness for me. To be so ill, yet so functioning.

Three full moons in the sky, equidistant to each other. One shines brightly, the other two are greyish green. It looks as though they are singing in a choir. They want the same thing, but they are not seeking support from each other.

Many times this autumn I have looked up at the tops of the trees, the bare branches, and believed it was spring; that winter is behind us. Then I remember, but it happens that I forget again. I look up at the sky and think, soon it's summer. It has to do with the eye, but not exactly with vision.

A parenthesis in time. The new (to me) experience of falling in love, finding myself in a mutual thing which then turned into aloofness, absence and distance. A relationship which doesn't quite end, but which circles around negations.

The days have passed. The season. My tree is in transformation, I am in transformation. The mole on the bottom of my eye: a tumour.

My seeing.

Willing myself to wait for you. And finally, my decision to stop waiting.

My tree is all trunk and bare branches. There is a magpie on the roof. No, now it's in the tree. I'm grateful for the existence of graphic birds. I can't miss the magpie. I'm grateful for black coffee in a white mug, for black letters on white paper.

Eric and his father who died last night. I said, now you don't need to think any more about how he couldn't give you love. Now he's dead and can't give you any love.

> Eric is my husband. *Now he's dead and can't give you any love.* I read the sentence again. Who is speaking here? If anyone understood the difficulties (and possibilities) of endings, even of death, surely it was Johanna? It's as if she is practising firmness.

I wake up thinking I am frightened. But *unsafe* may be a better word. Is it the same thing? I imagine someone taking my hand and leading me to the kitchen, the warmth of a hand on my shoulder through the pyjamas while I make morning coffee.

When I close my eyes to sleep, I see a green blinking light. I'm certain it's my mobile. Then I think it comes from the window. Then that it's a bulb failing, or a light from a fire alarm. It's strong and somehow sweeping, like the glare of a lighthouse. Then I understand that it's the eye itself creating light. It comes from inside; it's a light sweeping the inside of my eye. What is being illuminated? I sense a veined wall, a sandy bottom. I don't have time to see. I am blinded by the light. Then it's gone. I take slow, deep breaths. This will pass, I think. I must remain maternal in relation to my own body. What can I call the light to make it less frightening?

I dream that I am walking in S's garden at night. I see owls everywhere, small grey ones and some others, medium-sized. And then a great white one. Only I can see it. It sits in the birch tree, camouflaged against the light bark, but still visible against the dark sky. It turns its head.

I have dreamt about the tumour, about sight and distance. About how to calculate distance and about having been kept at a distance (by N). Tumours and gold. The blackness of the pupil. The tumour is the tumour: a thing. It has limits, it is possible to remove it. I almost never say cancer. And if I do, it's always with some caveat or excuse. Cancer is a condition. A tumour – an object.

One time I wrote a poem about birds sticking their beaks into my pupil.

I dreamt about a passage in an official building, maybe an airport. Aluminium, battered walls, high, dirty windows. Suddenly I see a bear outside. It presses its nose against the window. Further away a glass door opens and a keeper in overalls carrying a bucket comes in. But he doesn't close the door, he leaves it half open. The glass in the door is cracked. I don't understand why there are bears here, don't understand the carelessness around the door. A moment later the big bear is in the passage. It rocks slightly from side to side before moving towards me. I can't get out of the room but there is a ladder reaching the ceiling. It's a dead end. One can climb up, but not get anywhere else. But the ladder is so narrow that the bear can't come after me. I climb as high as I can, my head pressing against the ceiling, watching the bear roll on the floor with lazy menace. The bear says: *I am (much) bigger than you.*

The word 'passage' in the first sentence of this paragraph was originally 'room' – Johanna has crossed it out. Passage is a better word if you want to emphasise a sense of movement from a desolate public space to fear and dead ends. But I am more interested in the parentheses in the last sentence and the complex question of who is speaking, and how. A parenthesis is a difficult sign to convey even in a dream dialogue. And if the speaker is a bear, how complicated is the gesture – the speech – then? And what does it really mean that the bear is not just bigger but (much) bigger? Does it convert the story of the dream to a fairy tale? One thing we know about fairy tales: they always end well. Johanna was afraid. 'But listen,' I would have said, and did, in some attempt at consolation and then we would both cry at the thought of how unbearably hard this was and how much harder it would probably become.

It was about now that Johanna came to see me in England, for the first time since

Covid. I picked her up at the airport. My dog had thrown himself out of a ground-floor window to run after the car, and my husband rang me up to tell me what had happened. I misunderstood and for several seconds, phone pressed to my ear, I believed that my beloved dog was dead. Then Johanna arrived, my dog was alive, and she was alive, her eye was red and swollen and we laughed and cried and the other passengers quietly passed us by as though wading through deep water.

In Sussex with S. The therapeutic community. It is at this distance from my own home, in this break from motherhood, that I dream about the cancer, not just about vision and the tumour, the eye, distance. From this distance I can also remember myself as a teenager, see (with the help of S) a pattern to do with passion and idealisation. How I build up, then fall. A wholehearted love, unique and radiant, not least to do with language. And then the fall into desolation. Suffering . . .

I feel my tiredness, a gnawing hum through the body. I want to stay in bed. Sit in the chair for a long time, just looking, letting my thoughts grow quiet.

Yesterday I moved too quickly. I was febrile, walking into furniture, talking hectically. My mouth tasted of metal. T looked at me with scepticism and kept her distance until we hugged and held each other hard for a long time in the kitchen and I resumed the right shape and speed.

I wake up thinking that my bed must be wet with tears. In my dream I sobbed heartbreakingly. I was unprotected and despairing. I don't know who I was in the dream, but I had become attached to a young man who was a teacher, a leader, a trainer? Something to do with school and education. He was only here for a short while. Was he a substitute teacher? A guest lecturer with special expertise? I know he'll soon be done and then he'll disappear out of my life. There is nothing I can do about it. I have to let it happen. I have no say, he's not interested in my love. I forget to take my eye drops, my vision deteriorates. It's only an eye, I think. It doesn't matter. It's my heart that's sick.

The moment comes when he says goodbye. He can't see or understand the depths of my grief. I sob, saying nothing. I am a child and a grown-up. My self is constituted by a love which is everything but means nothing. I can do nothing with it, it's pointless. Maybe it's something else? The self is tears. He looks at me, says, *bye, then*, takes some postcards from his jacket pocket and gives me one. Maybe he got them on some trip and kept them in a drawer. Maybe he bought them on the way here? Did he spin a postcard rack, choose them with care? Did he pick them for me or because he liked them himself? The image is a flowering fruit tree. I take it in my hand. It's only a postcard, it's nothing. Still, I think I will dedicate a lifetime to interpreting its meaning.

I write down the dream again:

I dreamt about a young man I was secretly in love with. He was some kind of substitute teacher. When his term was finished and he said goodbye, I was inconsolable. He took a postcard from his pocket and gave it to me. He'd bought it on a trip, or someone had given it to him. It depicted a flowering fruit tree. I couldn't speak. Streaming tears. It would take a lifetime to interpret the significance and meaning of the image, even though in all probability it was just a random card.

There's something about the words today – they are not coming. It's as though they carry some underlying meaning to the effect that it's all worse – with me? With language, or with my ability to think? – than I had imagined. That it is precisely my capacity to imagine which is in a bad way.

I dream of battling a strong wind, and an equally strong wave. It hits me, I am blown to pieces, scraped bare. I move towards the impossible, both in thought and body. Whatever is not working has to work. And in the dream I don't tell myself that heroism, the impossible battle, has any value in and of itself. I don't tell myself that it would be better to find some other way, some easier and more welcoming path. In the dream I go to pieces.

At the beach some finds have been neatly lined up, skeletons, organs, muscles all arranged at precise distances. And then, further away, a bucket: I believe this to be language. But who is the I who sees all this? Where am I?

I wake up jaws aching, clenching my teeth. I am very tired. I can't manage my exhaustion. Or: I don't dare to.

It's happening again. I look at the bare tree and believe it's spring. It's not just a mistake in my mind, it's a mistake in my body. The same thing, to a lesser degree, happens when I wake up. The nights are never long enough. My sleep is like the anaesthetic. Time is cut up and pieces of consciousness are glued together almost seamlessly.

I was just thinking about Lilla Björka, Elin Wägner's house, and our writing residency that week in May. The lily of the valley had not yet blossomed. The buds were like pale peas. My walks, there, my rounds. So much was about allocating time. A few times we walked together. We were almost like a normal couple. I mean: a couple who jointly imagine a future life, and at least to some degree find themselves in the same life.

I remember that we laughed one evening. And that we sat close together watching movies on the laptop. But I didn't know where we were in time. Was this a parenthesis, a counting down, a great cramping repression?

You read what I wrote, but you didn't show me anything you wrote.

You took long, hot baths. There was something so private about you then that I couldn't even look at you. And of course, I knew that you didn't want to be seen. I could describe the atmosphere in that house in detail. An untraceable emptiness. A snarled-up machine. A jaw, locked. I had to ask for permission to touch you. When I stretched out my hand you backed away.

Very quickly and unnoticeably one forgets what normal life is like, and what is reasonable in one's own world.

My books are mirrored in the window. The façade opposite becomes a bookcase.

Further down the street there's a patch of green. There is a bare tree on a slope with a bird's nest in its branches. Under the tree and scattered on one side of the hill: yellow leaves. They are like candles. I remember the golden shimmer in my eye last summer. The glitter, the powder. Miniature fireworks, shining cascades. Now the gold shines under the tree. In the tree, the nest: my tumour.

T plays on her keyboard, singing: *You're a little much for me. You're a liability.*

I'm thinking about the concept of a storm petrel. An ominous sign. Not magic, rather something very matter-of-fact. I saw, but I wasn't frightened.

I write and cross it all out, it comes out wrong. It's not true. I experiment with language to get closer to the truth, but I lose speed and direction. I cross stuff out and feel embarrassed because it's obvious that writing is the safest act I can perform.

There is actually quite a limited repertoire of acts in everyday life.

Mum used to say, when she could still speak, that the whites of my eyes were so white they were almost blue. Now my right eye is red. In the white something is healing, leaving a little scar on the surface. I don't really want to look at it. Maybe it will calm down. The most likely thing: I'll get used to it.

November 8th, 2021. The first snow of the season. The cloud cover is thinning, there are blue patches between clouds drifting to the south. But behind the roofs opposite the colour of the sky is wet.

I'm hesitating to write down the dream. I don't want to remember it because when I woke up I believed for a moment that it was true, that I was in a reality impossible to get out of. I and N and B were in New York. N had bought an apartment on the Hudson. Was it ours? He didn't love me any more. A man with a bald and greasy head in a T-shirt, jeans and flip-flops quickly showed us around. The walls were roughly plastered and painted mint-green, pale ochre, light pink. I took the room on the right. A single bed, views of the river. The only light was a neon tube in the ceiling. The furthest room was unfurnished apart from a bed. B sat on the floor unpacking.

I didn't want to be in New York. I wanted to go home. When I asked N about the apartment his voice turned hostile and passive. No, he didn't know anything about contracts or agreements. No, he didn't know how much it had cost. I asked if he hadn't bought a flat in Stockholm, too. I could somehow visualise it: white walls, parquet floor. Two rooms in a modern building. I said: 'I don't remember what happened,' and immediately felt the self-dramatising lie in that statement.

The apartment on the Hudson was nightmarish, a big rough cave on the seventh floor. Everything was over between us, which is why I picked the small room with the single bed. And yet I felt a wish to be led to and be offered the double bed in the other room, N's room. I thought I would call Jakob, but I couldn't figure out the time difference. I also didn't want to give him the bad news. It was so chaotic and so crazy. Instead, I texted him: 'Do you know any good restaurants near the Hudson?' I knew, of course, that all we had to do was go out, find somewhere, no matter what. I heard N speak on the phone with a woman, then with a child.

I knew nothing about his life. I was cold with anguish. Those walls were not me. I recognised the inhumanity from somewhere. How you can function even though you are almost dead. I said, 'I want a lawyer. I don't understand where this money came from.' N took off his belt and tied it round us both. He was so determined that for a moment I mistook it for an act of love.

> I think of Isaac Bashevis Singer's novel *Shadows on the Hudson*. Life after the Holocaust, in New York. I had it out when Johanna arrived; we talked about it.

I dream I'm a teenager at Stora Skuggan. I have anorexia. I am cleaning the kitchen. My hands are blue with cold, the skin is dry and rough. In the cupboard under the sink there's a bucket and some yellow rubber gloves. When I try to put them on, I notice that inside the gloves is a pair of thinner gloves, the disposable kind used for painting. There is a rotten smell, and a greenish-brown liquid inside the disposable gloves. My parents never really take care of the real dirt. I am the only one to do that, and the cleaning lady who comes now and then. I want to do the cleaning. I have the vision and the capacity. And as long as I clean and cook and take care of the house and don't eat, I keep my story and myself alive. The story is about the fact that something is wrong, that someone is not seen or cared for. In fact, she is the one who takes care of others, but not with maternal care (she is a child), nor with a warm heart (she acts from a place of desolation). She feels pride. Her back is straight. And she doesn't dare give up. She has no idea what would happen if she did, but she has a sense of it: she would become like the house, like those gloves, rotten, stinking, hidden, because they are not compatible with the idea of happiness in that house.

For the first time in my life I dream that I am floating in space in a night full of stars. I see an airplane and a satellite. It is so delightful, so liberating, until I realise that I am alone, and I know I wasn't alone to begin with. There are two possible reasons for my solitude: I have been abandoned, or I have done something wrong.

I dreamt about me and my brother in a hotel room with our mum. The view is a snow landscape, blinding white. Mum has had her stroke; she is tired but functioning. Her scent, White Linen, is in the bathroom. (In real life I associate that scent with her heart operation when I was ten. A hole in the heart, the hospital, her fear.)

I am alone in the room. A swallow has flown in through the window and sits on a protruding socket high up on the wall. It's black, with a white chest. I slowly move towards it so as not to frighten it. I open all the windows, put on my dressing gown and go out into the snow, calling it to come with me. Suddenly it flies out and away.

Tall men with small dogs are walking. The hard crust of the snow glistens. I pick up a puppy and hold it to my chest. I feel tenderness, but I don't need to own it or take responsibility for it. The owner takes the puppy with the words: *I lift him in a bow saw grip.* I think maybe it's the way he puts his hand under the puppy's tummy that has to do with a saw. Or perhaps it's the puppy's bent shape as it is being held.

Mum is dying in the hotel room. She is breathing very quietly. Then she doesn't breathe at all, and she is dead. The grief I feel is the grief of a child, but it's also my grief. The child I once was fills me to the brim with her grief. Our grief.

From the rooftop over the crown of the tree and out of the image. The seagull. I wonder if their flight varies with sleep and food. Maybe an ornithologist would know. I wonder about my own eyes, my sight, my field of vision.

We swam in luminescence that last night by the sea. Sea fire. It was so beautiful that we just laughed. A special laugh made of joy and surprise, not humour. An open laugh before the elements. (Dearest, I so want you to remember it!)

Every now and then I see a very small blue dot like a star in the centre of my right field of vision. Same strength, regardless of light and dark. An electric glow. I think of Jarman's blue film. I imagine entering into the blue while it lasts even though the feeling is that it is out of reach. I would widen the opening, raise the stage curtains. Behind (or in front) all would be equally blue. And it would be like an ongoing but static end. An end without ends. A beginning without beginnings. The walls transformed into the world of emptiness.

I lean my face in my hands and feel my age. My skin is smooth, but so much thinner than I remember it. Perhaps I don't often let my face fall into my hands.

In the beginning I wrote in anticipation of you. At best, I conjured you up so that you would keep me company. At worst, I wrote through you to soften the fall. My fall. Lately I have written to understand myself better (and you, but it's guesses on guesses). What is this time called, and this act? Our obituary? A long afterword for a story that was really very short. There are elements here of romantic illusion. But there are other elements of illusion too, which frighten me.

I am finally beginning to understand that we are moving into winter, not spring. What remains of my delusion is that this year feels like a single day. The edges of time have been erased; the rhythm of time has been suppressed to one single beat.

Yesterday I saw the oncologist for the first time since the operation a month ago. I walked to the hospital. After the curve across Slussen and the streets of Gamla Stan, it's more or less a straight walk. It takes an hour door to door. As I got closer to the hospital my legs dragged; I felt a sudden exhaustion and didn't know if it was animal reluctance or some kind of anticipation of care. Did I want to cancel my appointment or did I want to be admitted and put to bed?

Patients from all over Sweden come to the eye oncology ward. I heard what I think was Tornedalian Finnish. A couple spoke Dalmål. One man seemed mentally ill, speaking quietly to himself – I think I heard him mention Ursa Minor and the Big Dipper. I wonder if he, like me, saw stars and constellations in his eye.

My tumour is irradiated and seems not to have grown. That is all they can say now. It is in the process of being destroyed. A dying volcano (always that need to find a visual language).

The consultant showed me the old image of the tumour, stretching against the macula, the yellow spot. The location caused my symptoms. The consultant said that if – against expectations – the tumour is still alive in some places it can be irradiated again from the outside. But if it has already reached the pupil, the head of the optic nerve where it exits from the retina, then the eye has to be removed. At that point the tumour could metastasise through the blood.

Yes, I can see that. Then it would be good to remove the eye. The consultant talks about an ocular prosthesis. I say fake eye.

I buy a saffron bun on the way home.

I have to watch my statements about myself.

I wrote a poem many years ago (decades ago) about a bird with its beak in my pupil. I have to find that poem.

At this point Johanna crossed out the following sentence: 'It was not deadly. It was an opening for the beak.'

The idea of the bird picking the tumour out of her eye had become a strong image for her. If the bird represents treatment, that might be what should have been done: remove the eye.

But the tumour had probably already started to send out cells for new colonies. I read the last notebooks and feel her subterranean panic.

Writing is my body. Reading is my house where my body walks around. I read what I just wrote and think it's sufficiently true.

Note: I have to come back to the art trip to Denmark/Louisiana. Copenhagen, and the terrifying unfreedom when I thought I would feel free. I was already abandoned and in need of home, not travel; the known, not the unknown. Everything was ugly and I was poor. My face was greasy. My body! These were the days just before going to the optician and then hospital. After that I couldn't look at my face or my body with dislike or discomfort any more. Brave body. Brave eye.

It will be fine. I will never again accuse my body of not being good enough. No more self-contempt, repulsion, evil looks. Let the least positive judgement be that judgement itself is uninteresting.

I dreamt I was in Copenhagen on my own. I pass a house down by the harbour where there's a stage for poetry and spoken word. It's full, the readings have already begun. I hesitate, standing by the door. There's a boxed-in screen on the wall showing videos of previous readings, and I see N in the audience. So he is not as ill as I thought he was. He listens intently, engaging in the readings. I see him clapping wildly, hands above his head, shirt unbuttoned. Chiselled collarbone, skin shimmering pale. But I see no joy in him, only frantic determination. He doesn't seem to have a connection with anyone else, but perhaps the connection is with the words being read, or the atmosphere of the place. Whatever he may be missing, it's not me.

I walk through the town, following a street by a canal. Idyllic houses, outdoor cafés, beautifully painted façades. But suddenly the pavement ends, replaced by huge chunks of rock. A terrible accident could happen here. I measure the distance between two rocks with a foot in the air, and realise it's too wide. To continue I must sit down and glide on my bottom. How could they let such a welcoming and picturesque street end in a precipice? I change my mind about carrying on, get up and turn round. This town is not mine. It makes me invisible.

I dreamt that you sit on a chair, I stand or sit opposite. You have almost lost your voice; it's very low and hesitant. You look at me with a seriousness bordering on hostility. You say: 'You couldn't give me enough . . .' The last word is inaudible. You try again: 'You lacked . . .' The last word is missing. 'I wanted you to . . .' Again, it's impossible to hear the last word.

A misunderstanding: that I would be able to control or restore something with my writing. That I would be able to somehow conjure up a happier place. But it's only as I write that happiness is conjured up. When I cease to write, the place of happiness ceases to exist. I know I exaggerate, or rather that I disregard all other forms of happiness – my daughter, above all else. Just this – her way of holding my hand last night before she fell asleep. Through her twelve-year-old hand I felt her infant grip. Time streamed between our hands.

To really feel time in that sense is not possible without love.

I look up from my desk believing that a catastrophe has just happened, is happening, will happen soon.

Last night, great desolation. Nothing held together. I dreamt about my mother. We have met another guest in the small boarding house where we are staying. He wants to show us around and we go for a walk. He is an oceanologist. Mum walks so slowly, dizzy and breathless on the steep paths. I hold her arm and take her hand where it's steep. I want to hear what the man says but I can't let Mum down. I also don't want him to believe that I'm like her. I'm playing a double game and it's exhausting. I make conversation and listen to the man while supporting Mum, smiling reassuringly. It feels almost impossible. But I know that it's precisely the impossible which is my only possibility. That is where I'm resurrected, where I am not lost.

> Oceanologist. I think about Freud, Koestler, the idea of the oceanic: death.
>
> Jarman's blue film. Raise the curtains to an end without ends.

BOOK 12: NOVEMBER 2021–FEBRUARY 2022

My medical notes from the time I was diagnosed in September state that I 'seem to have acclimatised' to my reduced vision. The reduced vision is at times referred to as the 'loss' of vision, which I think is about a particular field of vision where I see nothing at all. I like the word loss, as though vision were a leaf falling from a branch. Like falling out of love. The moment before the fall: something loosens, doesn't hold. It no longer belongs.

November 29th, 2021. Four swans fly over the roofs. I only see them for a few seconds. I wonder how they see each other, how they calibrate distance, height and direction? What do their wings sound like?

I am reading Carrère's *Lives Other Than My Own*.

I think I am reading Winnicott and Buber, but that's my brother's reading.

The swans – do they experience themselves as one

single body when they fly, and then later as solitary beings, if not individuals, when they land?

When my son was very young, he once said, 'Mum, when I die and go to heaven or I'm buried in earth or I'm reborn as an animal, then . . .'

I don't remember what was going to happen then, but I do remember wondering if the agnostic uncertainty I had communicated to him was in fact hard to come to terms with.

How do we envisage death without faith? Johanna was an atheist but she might have played with the thought that the individual is dissolved and resurrected in a collective body. Swans flying in formation over the rooftops.

And where would that collective self have been located? Maybe in Jakob, in Winnicott and Buber; in the comforting thought about the good enough mother and the *I* in dialogue with the divine *Thou*.

Is the mother good enough even if she has to disappear? The heavy burden for the child is to have to assimilate what is left, the inner shadow image of the mother, and to gain support from others.

To have to reflect on these matters is unfathomably hard.

December 4th, 2021. It snowed last night. All the branches of the tree are frosty white. The roof is white, the window frames are white. The sky is light grey dotted with dirty clouds.

My thoughts are silent. I'm working on other people's texts, responding and commenting, but in between I'm barely thinking. It's quiet. I don't remember my dreams. Woke up with the feeling that something doesn't make sense. Something is missing or lost. I have forgotten something, misunderstood, or been misunderstood myself. It's not acute. A slight glide. A mix of, say, homesickness and anxiety about having left home without blowing out the candles.

I search for the magpie in the tree. I don't see it, and imagine it. Then I see an abstraction of it (a sign). On the part of the black tin roof opposite which is laid vertically with joints making the roof striped (black on black), the snow, which otherwise covers the whole roof, has slid off. Four sections of black against the white: an illustration of the magpie! And just as I think I see snow falling from the top branch (a miniature snowfall) and the magpie rummaging around, head nodding as if to an invisible audience, it's all suddenly gone. I didn't see it fly off. It is a camouflaging kind of morning.

It was a day that tried to camouflage excessive approximation. Everything was a bit loose, things fell off, left me, or sabotaged my thoughts and actions. I thought, as I did when my back was painful: it doesn't happen often but it's still strange that I forget that I have it in me. The possibility of this happening. The risk.

At an Oneg Shabbat dinner at the Jewish Centre we discussed Jewishness as a screen for the projection of darkness, chosen people, community, trauma, mysticism and so on. The words linger in my mind. I think about what I projected on N, my own idealised image. A homecoming. This morning I will hold on to that for as long as it can comfort me. I wrote him a text yesterday when I was at my lowest point, telling him about the magpie and the sign of the magpie on the roof. For the first time ever, I hoped that he wouldn't respond. He has said it, he has no answers.

And I know: there are no answers.

Twenty years ago, I met a woman, Jocelyn, in LA. She said, 'It's easy for you to see the magic and attractiveness in others, but don't forget that others see it in you, too.' We exchanged some emails after I left LA. She answered less and less frequently until she didn't answer at all. I carried on writing until I found out that she was dead. I had written for a year to a person who no longer existed. For me she existed for as long as I was writing. And ceased to exist when I stopped writing.

The camouflaged day became less and less camouflaged. My brother helped me with some practical things. His family was here. We celebrated Hanukkah. They left. I tidied up, got T into bed. After a week of quiet nights, I had a nightmare. It was like drawing the curtains open one last time. Everything will be revealed at the point when you can stand seeing it.

I and T are on a boat in the archipelago. Our things – some of them are important – are packed in a flimsy raffia suitcase. T suddenly gets off at one of the stops and doesn't have time to get back on before the boat backs away from the quay. Terror courses through my body when I realise that I can't reach her or persuade the captain to turn the boat. I realise I must have patience and wait until the end station and then make my way back from there. But for how long will she wait until she gives up? Where will she go then? I imagine or see in my mind's eye a kiosk, some tables and chairs, rocks, stunted pine trees, the sea outside. A view altogether frightening. But what scares me most of all is the thought of her waiting, unoccupied. I wish so intently that she will have the courage to ask the person behind the counter for pen and paper so that she can pass her time drawing. It's the lack of occupation, the emptiness, which makes me feel so desperate. That is what I have to save her from. That's what I am going to help her with. It's a struggle against time. I don't want her to be frightened. But it's her resignation which makes me frantic in my efforts to reach her. If she gives up and becomes passive, apathetic, without thoughts or internal images she will be lost, and I will not be able to find her. I wake up feeling crazy.

Islands of reading (a book, my own unfinished stories, student texts, the film script of a friend) and writing: the unfinished stories, responses to students, comments and suggestions to my friend. These islands are tied together with coffee, text messages, laundry drying on the radiators, T's homework and lighting candles. Candles burning down, changed and lit again.

T is with her father. Mum-week is over. Last night I dreamt that I opened a parcel that had come in the post. It's hard to get the tape off, and I tear the paper. Some white powder spills out on my sweater and bare underarms and on the people standing around (who are they?). Apparently, the powder can give you cancer. You can become infertile. I think: that in itself doesn't matter. I already have a child, and I am too old to have a second. And there is no certainty that it will give me cancer. A woman next to me (is she my ex-husband's first wife?) says the powder is very strong and brushes it off my arms with a handkerchief. Says, feel that – your skin is so rough now. And I realise I never even for one moment thought I would get cancer.

I have been with my mother. She is dying now. I held her forehead against my cheek. She was a child. I was a child. I remembered the little maquette for a famous sculpture: a boy, sitting with his arms round his knees, face turned slightly upwards. She always had it within sight at home. I took it from the drawer of her miniature chest on the shelf, held it in my hand and put it in my pocket. I didn't want to ask her about it. To take it was a way of making her dying real, but also to express loneliness – the reality of loneliness. The dread I felt for so many years – always, really – about her loneliness. My anxiety about it, even though I knew she often chose it. And now the little boy is here, on a pile of books in my window. His presence is more ambivalent than I had imagined. Not the boy himself but everything that comes out when I look at him. It's as if I have become my mother, filled with death. Waiting for it to devour me in one way or another.

I dreamt about Mum at her work table. Typewriter, dictionaries, telephone. Her dark hair is in a knot, she's wearing glasses with brown frames and a white blouse. The telephone rings. She puts her hand on the receiver, lets it ring a few more times. Then she quickly lifts it, bends forwards, says something. It's as though she wants to catch a prank caller, unmask or get at the caller in some way. She speaks quickly, in fragments. The words are incomprehensible. Is she speaking backwards? Someone on the line says she is dead. And she knows that the person she is talking to is herself. The sentences reverse, pulsate and cut their way back into her mouth. That is how she dies.

I long for my grandparents' kitchen. I step over the wooden threshold painted blue, stand on the lino looking out of the window. The Christmas bunch of oats and rye for the birds is up, the shells of seeds a yellow circle in the snow. The kitchen smells of gingerbread, orange and chewing tobacco. The clock on the wall is ticking. There is a gurgle from the sink. It's so quiet. My grandmother is resting in her room; I can do whatever I want, be whoever I want to be. But I just want to stand here. I don't want to be anyone else.

Every molecule is compact with existence. Even absence is present.

I dreamt that Mum dies. I come into her room. The carer is on a chair next to her bed. She asks if I have ever seen a person die. I shake my head. 'Then you should know,' she says, 'that every part of the body develops eyes. Hands, upper arms and forearms, neck, back, thighs. That's so that we can close the eyes, so that all parts of the body can find peace.'

My eye is roaring. It's like pressing the flat of your hand hard against the eye then letting go. A flickering nebula without clear boundaries. A glittering, restless glimmer.

I can almost ignore it, but not quite.

The magpie comes, sits in the tree, moves on the branch, turns round and round. I see it out of the corner of my eye. But when I turn it's gone. It comes and comes. It flaps its wings. The magpie. It doesn't exist.

My mother died yesterday. I saw her the day before. Her eyes were black, then. She was in bed looking inwards or beyond me. She looked towards the door as though she was waiting for someone who was not me. When I put my hand on her forehead, she finally closed her eyes. But when I moved my hand, she opened them again. The staff moved quietly in the corridor outside her room. Someone whispered my name; said I was her daughter. I stroked her shoulder, moved the cover, touched her skin. Her shoulders slope inwards, like mine. But they are just skin and bone. 'It will pass,' I said.

In the evening, reading on the sofa, I see a little bug crawling up the wall. With my sick eye it is just a blurry dot, but my healthy eye sees a ladybird. It crawls upwards for a while, then loses its grip and falls to the floor.

I wait for the nurse who will call and tell me that Mum is dead. 4.50 a.m. she calls.

I answer emails, text messages, telephone calls. I answer. Soon there is no meaning left in my words. I do everything I ordinarily do, but I sense that something has been lost in my actions. A kind of hollowing out. Brittle bones. I think about N, and the depression. The loss of meaning. I look out over the tree, the façade opposite, the sky, almost clear, thinking about how you can draw colour from an image. Cyan, magenta. Yellow, black. What disappears, what emerges? My mother's skeleton under the skin when I touched her the last time before she was dead. My daughter's soft forehead. N's collarbone, the visible blue veins on his arms. I put body-memories, history and desire side by side. It feels like needlework. Grief and care.

Gratitude flickers.

I have to move slowly now, so I don't become overwhelmed.

I dreamt about walking on Canal Street in New York. Someone told me about a play that has been on for decades in a basement venue. It's a murder mystery with different outcomes. The person says: 'The solution to the mystery is in the title. The "O" can be read as a zero. Are you one of those who believes that? Or do you take it for granted that O and zero are two different things?'

Later I am in the small basement, and the play is about to begin. The auditorium is very steep. I make my way up the stairs. I have changed my mind, must leave before the curtain is raised. But the exit is blocked. I press against the door; it bulges slightly but doesn't open. I believe I can open it with force. Everything is connected in the difference between control and impulse. What is the right thing to do? The venue is a trap. The difference between an O and a zero. To be sceptical or credulous. I feel the door give way under my strength. But I wake up before I find out that I got out.

The handwritten O in Johanna's notebooks can in fact be read as 0. The origins of the symbols are the same, omega and omicron. They speak of endings.

Canal Street divides SoHo from Tribeca. If you cross it, you enter another part of town. Another world.

I dreamt that I see I outside the house. But she is dead. And yet I know it's her. I turn back, say her name. She turns away so I can't see her face. 'I!' I say and touch her shoulder. Unwillingly, she turns round. It's her but it's not her. The face is patched up, sewn together with rough stitches. The body is heavier, broader than her own. The velvet coat she always wore is made of leather. 'I!' I scream. 'You are dead!' She stares at me with cool eyes asymmetrically placed in her face. 'And Mum! Mum is dead!' I shout and shove her to make her disappear or to make me wake up. But before I wake up, I have time to shout one more time that Mum is dead and I weep like a child, I scream and cry.

I and my godson are cooking and drinking wine. My daughter is setting the table, then lies down on the sofa with her mobile. Everything is so intensely alive and simultaneous.

Late at night I and T fall asleep to an episode of *Friends* in my bed. I wake up, turn off the lights. I dream that my mother is dead and that I can't stop crying. Snot and tears, loud sobs, not quiet weeping. And I don't know if I am just her child, or if I'm actually a child. But I know that my tears are impossible for anyone to receive. A shard in me knows I am doing the wrong thing and that my parents disapprove. Neither of them step towards me. Instead: they step away.

> This is happening at our house. The godson is my son. It's Christmas.

The promise about my body is not holding. That it was a good body, strong, good enough. Beautiful, even? That from now on it was just going to be my own proud body. My disappointment that the promise to myself is as good as broken, on course to be broken, makes me want to notice and mark the change in myself. How could I have believed that I could promise myself a constant emotion?

From time to time, I stop breathing. That's to say, I take shallow breaths, and then I hold my breath. It's not a good feeling. The body. The soul. Not good. I am a ghost, heavy as lead. Every limb is useless. I hold my breath.

My brain, my thoughts . . . I don't believe my mother's body is just a body. She's turning black in the cemetery, still not buried, and I am like a frightened child who doesn't understand what's happening, and who doesn't want to understand. And I can't change it, I can't make it good, deny it or repress it.

T plays with her Tarot cards. I ask a question about

love and the future, and I believe everything she says. I analyse her answers myself. I hold my breath.

Deadly serious, I believe it all. It has something to do with me. Not magic, but my own capacity to churn out interpretations, to stretch meanings. If I can't do that, the meaning of the last card is too frightening.

It says 'death' on the card.

Is it Mum? Is it me? My death? No, it's about loss, about a removal, an empty space creating opportunities, maybe choice. *Something*, not someone, has to die. Everything is real. But I am uncertain about the meaning of 'real' now. The Tarot cards, my mother's body? Interpretations or facts? They say, 'She is not there.' I say, 'Yes, she is there.' Is that because I am so imprinted by my anxiety for her? Her loneliness? Her lonely body?

If I have metastases on the liver, I will love my body again. No one else will love it like I will. I imagine the moment with the radiologist. Whatever he says, I will answer: 'I knew it!'

Just now, at this moment, I don't have the capacity to think deeply. Have I become a child, believing that my mother is alone in her coffin in the cemetery? Rotting, turning into soil, because I am not there?

She is not dying. She is dead. She can't die. She is dead. Nor can she live.

Worms and bugs move in her. No, it isn't her. They move in the body that at one time was her. No longer. All this has to be written down, so I understand. This is my lesson. I mustn't make any mistakes. I want to get all the answers right, because one single mistake frightens me.

I am not used to feeling this slow or to not sensing some kind of future. It's there, but it's a dawning world. A world of dawn? A world of dusk? I say yes to both suggestions. And if it's a statement, I will say, 'I knew it.'

(What is it that I'm moving towards? My thoughts are those of a child. My body is like a big sack of compost. Wet and heavy and impossible to carry. I hold my breath. The sack will be emptied over my mother so that I can help her to escape. That last is an exaggeration. Not true. I have some bad days inside me. I am estranged, not as alive as I should be or as I would wish myself to be.)

What is that childhood fantasy, poem or dream about a bird sticking its beak into my pupil? I see a hummingbird, sucking nourishment from my gaze. No resistance: I wordlessly share something. But I am sharing with a being who doesn't talk, who can't convey anything to others. I don't want to think about that image any more.

I don't have many words. The body aches. Head, back, shoulders: a hard casing. When I finally relax, gratitude springs up. Let it always be just like this. And then laughter bubbles up, at the smallest thing. The emptiness and the laughter.

My dead mother. She was there. For me, she was there. I could have stayed forever. Maybe because my child wasn't there. I was just Mum's child. I and my mum. My dead mum. I didn't feel that she was dead. Didn't feel that her body was dead. Are the body and soul of mothers one? I loved my dead mum.

On the flight home with T I fall asleep. It's night above the Atlantic. Next to me is my mother, in the seat in front of us my brother, who is also my child. The captain leaves the cockpit and passes by, saluting air hostesses in red and dark-blue uniforms. I think: this is what the world looks like. We are . . . above the world and even here the order of hierarchy is intact.

It looks festive. One could be tempted to believe that it's a form of ironic entertainment. On the windows are runnels of rain, sharp sunshine, deep-purple thunderclouds.

Suddenly the plane takes a sharp turn. The pilot announces that we are trying to avoid a thunderstorm. The body of the plane vibrates, the wings shudder. A moment later we are in the storm. We are in an impossible small space within it, hurricane winds and thunder all around us. I am not afraid until suddenly I am afraid. We are crashing, not forwards but backwards, nose of the plane high in the air. It's a great effort to lean forwards in the sharp angle, but I have to hold my child who is my brother who is both. I stroke the child's arm, hold his shoulders and I know that my hand is relaxed, that I can make my body fearless while my thoughts have already begun to scale down. Soon we'll die. Meanwhile, I will not show fear. Nor can we be together in death. I experience the loneliness of catastrophe, of accident, of death.

Mum touches my arm but she means nothing now. The only thing I can do is communicate non-fear to my child. I slowly stroke his arm and shoulder while the plane crashes backwards and we are sucked into ever more vibrating speed. It's soon over. Soon it will be over.

I wake up and I'm terribly afraid. I feel the taste of panic, I can't breathe behind my mask. It's black outside, the cabin is unlit. I have vertigo and must breathe deeply. I think about the relationship between pain and fear.

I think about my dead mother and about my mother.

I think about the tumour in my eye which is alive or maybe dead.

I think about the airplane, the vulnerable maternal body in the eye of the storm.

> The maternal body of the plane in the eye of the storm, the child who was also the brother.
> The maternal body shudders.

> Imagine waking from a nightmare about a plane crash in a dark airplane.

> Imagine waking from a nightmare about death in the knowledge that a tumour behind your eye may be alive or may be dead – and that if it is alive, it is most probably deadly.

Stockholm, January 10th, 2022. Today we are burying Mum. It's the first day of spring term. The snow on the roof opposite looks as if it has both fallen from above and been blown from the side. It's dark. Some illuminated Christmas stars still hang in a few windows. The white patches of snow on the black roof make me think of slipping.

A child drunk with sleep in the back seat without a seatbelt hits her forehead on the driver's seat, bites her tongue.

Yesterday at the cinema with T my back was so painful that for a while I was actually afraid. I thought, this is the only disadvantage of being alone with her: if I become acutely ill, she will have to see it all, feel it, act in solitude, experience her own vulnerability and mine, and love me until she hates me for it.

The snow on the roof is the same kind of snow as on the road outside Stjärnan, my grandparents' house in Västmanland. Snow blown from the ditches, from the ploughed fields and the meadows. Snow against asphalt. Now it's snow against black tin. I'm pinching time like dough between my fingers.

I express myself like my mother. The dead author, 'who, in 1996, was silenced'.

I dream about N. A last goodbye. Something to do with a common origin. Mixed woodland, a few aspens, last year's grass. A pale sky. An old schoolhouse is now a literary centre where people write, attend lectures, learn about beatnik poetry, Baudelaire, I can't remember. Bright classrooms, unpainted wooden floors. We walked amongst the sparse trees. I wondered if I could live with someone who doesn't have the energy to meet me halfway, to look up and meet my eyes. But I didn't want to leave him. It seemed like he was my responsibility, the price I was meant to pay. Someone pointed out the impossible nature of the relationship, someone else said I was the only one who could determine the cost, the pain. Someone asked if my goal in fact was hardening myself. Someone else mentioned my anorexia and the capacity to be content with very little.

We were on our way to the schoolhouse. I had wanted to hold his hand, but it avoided mine. I had wanted us to walk with our arms round each other. Our soft skin. It hurt a bit, as always. I said nothing and didn't try to get closer to him. I knew that the pain would get worse if I suggested or asked for something and the answer was no, the movement evasive.

That pale, faceless rage under the skin.

But still I felt a sudden jab of joy. I was strong and imaginative. N was my ongoing fantasy. My sweet possibility. I saw him as I had always seen him – more clearly than anyone else. My invisible boy, my twin, my guy, my playmate and my lover. Beloved.

This was the landscape of my childhood. An existence of lonely fantasies about a large and warm life. A life of grand gestures but also of grown-up safety, which was hard even to imagine other than as certain colours and structures. I knew too much about abandonment and aloofness. I fantasised my way into a sense of my own value. I dreamt up a boy who loved me, who was intelligent, reliable and inventive, who smelt so good and who was there for me. Someone who wanted only me. And that fantasy made me feel at home and authentically myself.

I dreamt that I was writing autofiction with leftovers instead of with words. I'm in a house with large windows facing the sea and the sky. People are moving through the rooms. I'm doing things with the leftovers: a bit of pasta, sundried tomatoes, some grilled vegetables in a pan. A friend of a friend, a familiar face, crouches down next to me to 'read' what I have 'written'. I explain that the story is about us, and yet not about us. That

I changed the names. He says he doesn't understand. He is an actor. Then he eats the food, the text. A while later he throws up on the carpet. I leave the room, pretending it has nothing to do with me and my text. A friend cleans it up with a wet rag before going down to the sea to wash herself.

I bite off a tooth. I see the image of icebergs calving at night. *Calving.* That actually is the term. The little things. But the cold, too. The cold calf.

I am frightened at the dentist's. I wasn't afraid of my eye operation or the radiation, but I am afraid of the drill, the nerve sensations in my jaw. The intervention in, or inside, my face. I want to cry.

At home I fall asleep on the sofa. Four times I go to the kitchen to get painkillers. I come back to my chair with 1. a box of matches, 2. nothing, 3. orange segments in a cup and 4. nothing. My helplessness or need of help glides around like air bubbles in oil.

Longing. I look out into the dark, in the country. I am a child. I see two moving dots of light. A pair of walkers carrying torches. I open the window, almost burning myself on the radiator. The cold streams into the room. Now I hear snow squeaking under their boots. Coats rubbing against each other, a swishing sound. I hear voices, but not what is said. People, an evening walk. It's as if precisely that image is as good as a painkiller.

I don't want what I am experiencing now to be about my mother's death. But everything is about that. Not always with the fact of her death, but with the fact that she was my mother.

I dreamt that someone said, 'It's my place, I know it. Every stone and bush, every tree trunk, every path to the sea. But even so there are sides, always sides or dimensions that remain unknown. If I deviate even in the slightest from the path the known becomes almost unknown. Everything changes. *Everything*, meaning me. You do understand that I am talking about grief? Or love . . .'

Philosophical questions about death are not important. Objective realism is the only important thing. Realism and all the rest, the secondary stuff. The primary thing is T. How will she be taken care of? How will she move through life; grow and age? Her movements . . . I want to make sure it's all choreographed in a way that doesn't harm her. An example I just thought of: if I die soon, it's important that our flat doesn't become a deceased estate. She has the keys. She opens the door. She goes to her room. She's alone. The things will seem alien to her – that is to say, my things, my books. She is too young to have integrated them or to have created a certain distance from them. Well, she uses some of my make-up and creams. Sometimes she borrows a sweater that looks cool and oversize on her. I don't want her to be here without me, in what might become an unexpressed desolation.

But most of all the desolation is mine. I was born with it. She was not. But she might grow into it, or it might grow in her.

Open question: optimism which does not turn into naivety. Thoughts about death which I must welcome but also reject, like guests whom I have to get to know for strategic reasons without particularly liking them. They go, but they leave shadows. Is that too metaphorical? Say, then, that there are thoughts, a language which falls quiet but continues to rumble under the skin.

I dreamt that my sister-in-law's little poodle could speak. Well, she knew that it had learnt a few words, but I could perceive whole sentences. My stroke-trained ear discerned consonants in what otherwise sounded like a slightly hesitant howling. 'How did you learn to speak?' I asked, even in the dream conscious that I had spoken to a cat the night before, who had understood what I said without itself being able to speak. The dog nodded towards a box of pencils. There were only a few pencils left, the rest he had eaten. Language resided in the pencils.

My sight is getting worse. Scars are forming. I can still see a bit with my bad right eye, but in the left field of vision there is darkness. Does the darkness exist, or do I see it? Is it my experience, my subjective reality?

Also: seen from a distance people have quite small heads.

I no longer pour coffee next to my cup. I don't misjudge distances. Sometimes light sweeps across my field of vision when I close my eyes. If I open my eyes, I can still see it. It doesn't end suddenly – it must run its course. A light. Not useful. Other than as a reminder.

Last week I thought about death until I was saturated with it, tired and nauseous. It reminds me of being pregnant – that vague nausea which you can only combat with eating. Is it physical or psychological, what I feel now? It comes over me as I write. Vertigo starts in my stomach and rises like fog.

Aimless snow over the black roof. It's not freezing. I have warmed croissants in the oven. T is watching *Friends* in her bed. At times she laughs her surprised and open laugh. The recorded laughter sounds like synthetic sparkles in comparison.

I suppose the fear is not dangerous exactly, but it's easy to misunderstand it. It makes me sharp. Then it makes me tired. I understand the sharpness, but not the tiredness. Seriousness is good. Pessimism is uninteresting, it doesn't speak, but nor is it quiet or rich in visual images. Grim severity tastes acidic. Denial tastes like paper. But anxiety is nauseous. The nausea is like an omnipresent, almost inaudible note. Like the sound of a fan, which when you turn it off gives you the freedom of silence, a larger room.

A little blue light, no, a little blue hole. As if reality were a cinema screen. Like my trouser legs, like the night sky just now, seen through the windowpane. But the light isn't a tear in reality. It's a scar in my eye, in my field of vision. The blue reminds me of landing strips at airports. The blue lights, my favourites.

In the far corner of the field of vision of my right eye something trembles and shakes like a grey, cold day by the sea. Rain like pale pine needles in the air; lines or stitches.

I read and the letters get tired, somehow bleeding.

The sea keeps its silence. The sea is rising.

I will take all the stories and the words I know and all the love I know and spread them out without losing them. They will become small, shining fragments of a large, loose weave which I will wrap myself up in, which will comfort me in my dying. More than anything I am thinking about wind in the sails; the difficulty of breathing when you have to do something against your will.

My will has been witnessed. The only important thing if I should die within the next few years is that T is taken out of the flat. She has to somehow make her way out of my death without forgetting me.

What else? Nothing. (Enough said.)

The sound of a snowplough far away. A harsh clatter with elements of squeaking. The magpies – a pair – fly between the tree and the gutter.

Sometimes sadness looks like love. My stomach and chest are filled with images generated by the snowplough. A scale of greys with elements of bright orange, blue and blinding white.

We all see with a subjective eye, depending on whether we have seen the scene before and what it meant in relation to the present. The moment I see, I also experience a memory, a mood, an experience hidden behind another experience. I speak to my gaze as though it were the loneliest gaze. But it's only a part of me. My words are the beginning of a dialogue. The gaze is invisible. But the experience of what the eye sees makes me visible.

I see friends. Intense conversations make for nights free of dreams. When I have an evening on my own with books, notes and wholewheat spaghetti with ketchup (my favourite!), then the dreams about death come. I go to bed, read the newspaper culture sections on the apps. I fall asleep. Then find myself in narratives where death is the basic premise. And death, in my dreams, intensifies my grief and love. I wake up. It's three or four in the morning. I am never afraid. I am heavy with grief and love.

I get up, pee, drink water. Fall asleep again and dream about death. The basic premise.

Just like the body generates hunger, thirst and needs from sleep, the body also generates death.

Death is me. Life is me. Just like the hunger is mine.

I dreamt that I was at an opening for a group show and the launch of an art magazine called *Boom*. The party takes place in a rough industrial space and 'Boom' is sprayed on one of the walls in red letters. An artist, sounding like a market vendor, calls out, 'A souvenir! This may be the last time you see Johanna. Boom!'

I flee to an adjoining room. It's empty and sunny, the walls are sooty black. A man in shabby clothing, a shaman or a priest of some kind, shows me a root, or maybe a tree stump, where I am to sit. He shuffles around me, speaking about the oak/*ek* in my last name. Am I sitting on a dead oak?

I enter other rooms. People are mingling, known faces, familiar from the past. There's no one I want to speak to. Yes, it's a show, and I am going to die. What do I have to say or speak about, other than that? But what if I am not? What if I carry on living? Then I've acted out, put on a drama in an ugly, egocentric way. Coquettish, exaggerated, melodramatic. The shame of that, the anticipation of shame.

In the dream I rethink my death: I can't be cremated, then I won't see T again. I must turn into earth, to worms. As a worm I can wait for her. Worms have no sense of time. I'll wait for her for eighty years and then we will see each other again. The thought calms me. We will see each other again as worms. Everything will be fine. There will be a happy ending, or rather, life never ends, and that *is* the happy ending. But then it occurs to me that T won't find me. How will she know it's me? Oh yes, I will shine like a red lantern. I'll be the only one. Rudolph the red-nosed reindeer. My red muzzle. We know the song by heart, sang it together last Christmas. That will be the sign. She will understand.

January 20th, was Margareta's memorial. Johanna and I walked in Tantolunden in the sun and snow and she told me about that dream. The worm, the lantern. Death. The thread connecting her to T. I held her arm in a tight grip, the ice was slippery on the path. She screwed up her eyes, turned her face to the sun.

After the memorial she and I and Jakob had pizza in her flat. Johanna was tired but we stayed talking for a while. She and Jakob were on the sofa, I was in the blue chair, where she had put up her feet. The memorial in the beautiful old greenhouse at Rosendal gardens was over, all had gone well. We had done what we had set out to do, and now we laughed helplessly at life, life, life.

The precarious days and nights in September before the ultrasound of the liver were short, cubical, metallic and methodical. I was prepared, stood to attention. Now I no longer stand to attention. My dark, glossy liver rests in me like a ray half hidden in sand at the bottom of the sea. At the bottom of the eye, the tumour collapses. Scars form. It's a whole landscape in there, not a metaphorical space.

I dreamt about BM's two budgerigars. She had dyed them red with ecological plant-based dye to match her hair. The female was B, the male M. BM was writing, and they sat quietly facing the other way, with their eyes closed. Then a falcon came and killed them. They died at 7.45 a.m., someone said. But BM did not agree. They only died an hour or so later. But the other person objected, saying, 'It is the exact time of death which counts.' BM answered: 'The falcon is not death.'

I dreamt about Mum. She is in a wheelchair, but she hasn't had a stroke, she can speak. I know that she will die. Perhaps she's already dead but I can still reach her. 'Mum, when you are dead, I will miss you. I love you.'

'Don't cry,' she answers.

The scene repeats itself, but slightly differently: a house in the country, summertime. My grandmother sits under the apple tree. I bend forwards to hug her, but I know that she is dead. She is not there. Mum sits next to her. I cry and cry until I dream; until I sleep. I dream and sleep from crying. Mum wakes me up. I say: 'When you are dead, I will miss you.' And I know that she will die now, that this is a farewell, and it reminds me of all the goodbyes of my childhood. I, who could influence so much with my will, my ability, my hubris, could never prevent my parents from travelling. It wasn't just the fact of their leaving that was frightening, it was the fact that I could do nothing about it. Now she is soon dead, now she is dying, and I can say those words of love even though I know it's too much for her, that it might cause her pain.

I was on my way to Israel, but my last Covid vaccination will only be valid in two weeks, so I stayed here. The days are quiet. Unusual. New. Days for writing. It's evening and I have written on unnumbered A4 paper in a large and childish handwriting.

I have read for hours, two novels, very different from each other. I read, holding my right wrist. A sense-memory of N emerged in the room, perhaps brought out by the two fictional protagonists. His forearms. The skin on my wrist and the bone, the bone under the skin. Touching myself is like touching him.

I let go of my wrist and feel very tired and very clear: I want to make everything good again. Get him a diagnosis. That's complex, but not hard. Medicine and therapy. The possibility of closeness, conversation, physical touch. I want to make phone calls, write emails, arrange appointments. Put patient documents in plastic folders and A4 envelopes. I want to collect, to clarify. And I want it to be put right. Is that even possible? It's not my responsibility, it's a manic desire for order. But it's also an acute wish to tell the story of . . . the brevity of life, and how real it can be. About the magpies in the tree and all that. Life as movement. The brevity of it all.

There's an apple core in an empty glass next to me. The evening is humming. I think so much about my friends, how they move, think, what they taste in their mouths. Their experience of the present, the evening, their routines which they pay attention to or ignore, thinking about other things. Soon we'll all sleep.

I think about their temperature. That we are in the same warmth even though we are in different rooms.

I am such a sucker for a happy ending. I always believe I can turn sadness to joy. Maybe that's why I write. Because something about writing is the opposite of the fine-print thin-skinned way of seeing. There is something about writing which involves twisting and turning, biting off and breaking up. The stubborn crazy wish to make the broken whole. To make the undoable doable. The unmovable movable.

> *I am such a sucker for a happy ending.* Sucker. She wrote it in English. Good word. A wave of missing Johanna courses through me as I write 'good word', her expression. We said it often as we talked about each other's texts. *Sucker* is a good word because it's so unpretentious, so real. Happy endings. It's that simple.

I think in the text I write. When I shut the notebook there are no thoughts left. Nothing to gain or to leave behind. I live in books. Completely and fictitiously. It's possible that I could remain awake and reprieved if I just carry on reading.

Two years since our dog died, and I still can't touch the memory of my daughter's grief. It burns me. But still her grief and how she handled it is something I am so grateful for, and proud of. Proud more than grateful, but I'm not sure about that word. Pride and grief; the words detract from each other. Something too hard in relation to something softer and bigger. This – babbling about words – is another sign that I can't handle it. But what I see is how she puts her fingers inside the dog's mouth to touch her sharp teeth one last time. Touch her inside the mouth. It's one of the most beautiful things I have ever seen in my life. She was a child, and she knew what to do.

Later she screamed and cried. She worked her way through the first pain and it was like giving birth, the waves of pain. I and her dad (I had asked him to come over) held her through the waves. She screamed: 'She will not come back!' And: 'I will never see her again!'

It's almost impossible to write this.

She articulated what death is. The most difficult thing about death. The only difficult thing.

BOOK 13: FEBRUARY 2022–X

I wake up and feel relief about the safe dreams last night. No information to be digested, no intrusive images to be endured. A patron of the arts in a grey suit offers prosecco. He takes my hand. I withdraw it but smile conspiratorially. A DJ who doesn't like prosecco asks to see the drinks list. There are palm trees in pots, white canvas, rickety bar stools. Staff in black and white. The whole place can be folded up and moved within an hour. The staff will return to school or university and then see each other again at the next art fair or cultural festival in town.

The DJ apologises, says he needs something strong. He has just made a playlist which took all night, he listened to hundreds of songs, often just a few seconds of an intro. 'A whole night of cuts of music, parts of sounds. You must long for silence,' I say. He drags his finger along the drinks list, says, without looking up, 'No, but I do long for a whole song.'

February 18th, 2022. The sky is so light and clear today that I briefly get vertigo. A May sky. Assertive, present, promising. The kind of sky that makes you euphoric. Or tired. Maybe embarrassed – one wonders how to live up to it. As if one could!

Every morning we should live up to the sky. The candles turn pale and fretful in the draught from the window and I blow them out. There is something behind the feeling I have now. A scream, tears, or a fantasy about redemption. A big feeling, too big to carry alone. But of course that's not true, it is possible to carry it alone. It's the fear of pain and even change that makes it hard for me to cross that border.

T came home from choir practice the day before yesterday and sang a song by Laleh:

> *En stund på jorden*
> *En stund på jorden*
> *Jag var nära, jag var nära*
> *Jag var nära, jag var där*
> *En stund på jorden*
> *En stund på jorden*

A moment on this earth
A moment on this earth
I was close, I was close
I was close, I was there
A moment on this earth
A moment on this earth

She sang and I felt the thin membrane between that which was and something else. Not the temporary movement, the awkward or accommodating tearful look, but something bigger. A grief indistinguishable from joy. The origin of despair. A love that is identical with pain but also with strength. Something impossible, like a scream louder than myself. A wish, a wish for life beyond myself.

I pushed it away and felt a nerve, a movement in my chest.

I pushed that away too and felt a breath of rage, almost humiliation, about it all. For being rendered, just for a moment, out of play.

(When she sings, she is the song. She is not someone who sings. Before she goes to school, I will tell her that.)

What can you expect of a day?

Sunday morning: the street is desolate. No people and no animals. A thin membrane of frost makes the pavements look like summer, the asphalt mild and dusty, a lukewarm vibration in the air.

A fleeting thought: that the buildings have emptied, been evacuated during the night. We are the only ones left. As if I had missed important information, slept through distress calls and signals.

Gaga online class with 900 dancers from fifty countries dancing in kitchens, in bedrooms, in living rooms and gyms and offices.

The feather that falls – light as a feather
The feather that falls – wet and heavy
The feather that falls – and sticks to a surface
From bouncing the feather away in the dance to carrying a headdress of feathers.

To be able to experience freedom. I have danced Gaga so many times now, and yet I tend to forget the joy in my body. It runs out, then it's resurrected. But it's hard for me to remember it. As with sexuality, desire. It's hidden.

I danced and I was concentrated, coquettish, self-conscious. I compensated with smiles. And later I thought that it was *right*. That is my tool. The tangible communication with the body. It felt unusual. Like hitting false notes and experiencing them as beautiful.

A game with the body that turned into language. And who was I revealing myself to? No one. I played, I shone, for no one. But the whole day I have carried openness in my body. The movement in the room. The attention to distance, front and back.

My words are my friends. That has not always been the case.

As I write it's as though the words give me presents, offers of associations, reminders of my own capacity to associate. It happens just as the words turn into writing and I read it. That moment of creation when freedom is at its greatest.

The tree shakes and rocks like a dancer. The view is colourless, the houses opposite mute. Only the roof tempts me: matt, clean after the snow melt. It's hard to imagine greenery, that transparent spray of yellow-green budding. I write it, so I think it. But I don't feel the greenery. It doesn't do anything with me. Instead faces glide past the window, projections of those I love. I sit and look at them, but we can't reach each other, and I don't even know if that is the point. Maybe the faces are thoughts. They are like fish, gliding past my diving mask. So close, but on their way somewhere else.

Lately, I have been almost as I was before. I feel joy of life in my armpits and neck. That is also me. Thoughts of death continue, not as a series of anguished questions but as factual findings, as one of many possible plans in life (life!), like the idea that I and J will travel to Safed in the Galilee; that I will write a play, or dance Gaga in Lombardy. And then eventually I'll die and that may happen in a year, or in three or five years' time? Maybe it won't happen. Maybe I'll live for a long time until I'll die as an old person. Not old-young as I am now, but aged.

I think of T, how well it will go for her, how she will carry the loss, wounded, healed and honed. How she will grow, carrying memory and an empty space. How she will take care of her life. I think it will go well. In fact, more than well. If I allow the future to be shrouded in the right shades of dark, light will gather here.

On February 23rd Johanna sees N again. He comes to the flat, they sit close together, she feels his presence but also his absence.

He suggests that we can see each other 'like this'. But 'like this' feels dark and slippery. We hold each other loosely for quite a long time. Then I stand, arms by my side, smile and say, 'Bye, then.'

At night I leave a house where there's a party. I walk in the sand between creeping pine and juniper on the way to the sea. Dawn is coming and there's a haze over the water. I walk in, swim a few strokes parallel to the beach. The water is shallow, but it feels good.

Suddenly it's impossible to get to shore. I struggle against the current, but the sea is stiffening like setting jelly. I see how hollowed out the beach is. The sea is unreliable, headstrong.

I make an enormous effort to reach the beach, which is suddenly at chest level like the edge of a swimming pool. Then the scene shifts. I look for something to grab to heave myself out of the water. Something that can hold me, tolerate my weight, carry me. I am a child, groping across white wallpaper. There! A cord. But the cord is pulled out of the socket and a table lamp, the lampshade creased, dusty, a little burnt, falls to the floor. There! A piano leg. I know it's heavy. But it's on wheels made of brass. It slowly rolls towards me until I let go. My arms are not strong enough, I don't have the technique to heave myself up.

My greatest help now is the strength that comes from my own fear.

Today the sky is more beautiful than . . . Than what? Itself. The clouds are a school of fat flounders.

I have to write to stop being this sad.

A black tin roof on a house by the sea. Volcanic rock all around, porous and sharp, impossible to walk on. There are narrow, paved paths. The sea almost reaches the house. Yes, it's an old harbour, but there are no boats. Something is moving on the roof. The loss of sight in my right eye means that I can't judge distances. Is it snails? Pigeons? Rats? No, it's pigs. They run around elliptically, at times dangerously close to falling off the roof. Their feet clatter and scrape in the gutter. They are sweet, but it's dizzying, frightening, to see them run so high up. Won't they slip, and die? Could they have been born there? They don't seem bothered by their circumstances, but it also looks like an insane prank. Most of the piglets are black, almost invisible against the roof. A small group are pink. They are chasing each other. Are they biting each other in the tail? Even though it's not that far away, I can't hear them. They play in silence.

Suddenly one of them slips, glides over the edge, falls on the volcanic rock and disappears between the rock formations. Maybe it's swept out to sea. It's torture to see it, to think the thought. But after a while I see the little pig cautiously trotting over the stones. It must be hurt, but I see no blood. Is that because it's black, so the blood is invisible? Or was the blood rinsed off by the sea? Or is it my bad vision?

It can't get up on the roof again to join the others. This is the beginning of a new life, if it survives. A moment in the middle of a game and then everything changes. A stretched-out *now* becomes history, the past, not the present. However recent it was it's still as far away as a childhood memory.

Was that my truest dream about the cancer? About death?

When N 'disappeared' I was struck down, entering into an acute period of unhappy love or even grief so intense that at times it was similar to being in love. Then it turned into a period of waiting, sometimes hopeful, sometimes anguished, other times completely quiet. I kept watch, inside and out. Perhaps grief is a form of compulsive waiting, and waiting, when prolonged, almost a form of grief?

Then I got my cancer diagnosis and waiting took on yet another form. An existential pause. I can't see the future as I once did. I saw it as a fantasy landscape, concrete but not real. Now I don't see that time as a place. And of course, the future only exists in our imagination. But if I open that door it's as if something tries to shut it again. A force as strong as I am.

I stand on both sides of the door. Sometimes I open it and then I am blinded. But shortly after that it closes, and I am the one who closed it again. That vertigo, that light, suddenly has the opposite effect. It's treacherous, only there to strengthen what I can't control.

I pray. Who am I praying to? No one. I wish, I beg, for seven years. Then T would be twenty. Seven long years. Am I greedy? So much time, so many days.

Three. I wish for three years.

Tomorrow, ultrasound of the abdomen. I refuse to articulate the word. Abdomen. A terrible word, swollen, masculine, blind. I have to think of the abdomen of an airplane to make it good. The smooth silver body filled with fuel and bags. But now my thoughts go to fighter jets and bombs. The world breaking. At the same time: it's International Women's Day. T is singing in church, and then I have tickets to a performance at the national theatre. I will go alone. A four-hour performance. I had acute back pain yesterday, maybe I can stand at the back after the first act. Thoughts, plans, things to do, the concentration in the dreamy state which has taken over and steered my life in the last few weeks. Yes, I am a mum, I speak, I listen. But it's as if a fog has descended, a haze slowing me down. A silence in my mouth, watchful sleep. I keep everything inside and at a distance. I have become a skilful sleepwalker.

I had bought a ticket for the performance in a year's time. I was 365 days too early for the play *Time Is Our Home*. The evening before the ultrasound.

Row eight, will I be there in a year's time? Alone, or with a friend in the stalls? It's as hard to imagine as anything else. So many of my fantasies are about memories. Recycling experiences.

Something repeats itself, but in a different light.

How can I write about this for myself, and at the same time make it a text for others? Again, recycling.

Another light.

The radiologist stopped the probe, then moved it in ever-smaller circles. The last time we had joked about my flat stomach, talked about cinnamon buns. 'No, that's not where they land on me.' He said he ate a cinnamon bun every day but also cycled to work. He had a central European accent. His eyes were smiling above the mask. I asked if he knew something he couldn't say. I also said that I knew he didn't have to answer. I didn't have any metastases, he said. 'You and I will see each other again in six months.'

I went out into the sunshine and cried.

Now, six months later, the same radiologist. He left the room without making eye contact. I knew, but there's still a difference between knowing something wordlessly and hearing the words seven hours later. 'Many multiple metastases in the liver, the biggest sixty millimetres in size.'

My heart rushed for a moment. Then indifference, quiet. I lay on T's bed and felt her smell as rings of years through time. Beneath her deodorant and girl scent was the smell of her neck, her hair, as a baby. It was all there, in one breath. A scent going back thirteen years.

To articulate this without self-pity is impossible. The words themselves carry the potential for what I may or may not feel. The treachery of language: it leaks and stretches.

Yesterday I wanted to write about the black-headed gulls. Their sound makes the air visible. I didn't see them, but I heard them.

I am in a lot of pain. It's hard to breathe. I can walk some 100 metres with small steps, but I can't talk at the same time. The liver is enlarged and hard as a stone pressing against my stomach, lungs, ribcage.

Metastases and necrosis in the liver. Metastases in the pelvis, on the pelvic bone. I have four days before I see my oncologist to learn about possible treatments. I had imagined coming to the appointment with the words 'I am strong as a lion.'

But I'm not strong as a lion any more. I can hardly stretch out my arm to reach my glass of water by my bed.

I have told T. Now everyone knows; friends, some acquaintances, the teachers at her school.

I want to live five more years. Then she'll be eighteen. Am I greedy? Two, then. That is so much time.

I saw T and her half-brother at my ex-husband's place. I have seen it before, but I have never been so struck by their mutual openness. It's as though they are huddling under a blanket of integrity, their bodies free and playful, their language annoying, teasing, loving. I watched them, and I watched my ex and I felt that this will work without me.

Eight days ago, when we almost missed a play in Vällingby, we ran along the platform and continued to run across the square. Not very far, but I did run. Yesterday, when I walked up the stairs to my neighbour who is a doctor, I stood for a long time catching my breath before ringing her doorbell. I stood leaning forwards with my hands on my knees searching for an angle where I could take a deeper breath.

I dreamt that I snuck out at dawn and walked along a narrow lane between rows of houses and gardens concealed by walls. It smelt of wet stone and greenery. The paving stones were dark, still damp from the night. I was able to walk! I walked quickly, took deep breaths. I breathed in and out. I was so content in my body. The sleep of the night was on me still like a membrane over my face. I felt my clothes touching my skin. There was the sea, and in front was the square with the market. At the far end, the cafés and the yellow merry-go-round.

It was morning now. The market was in full swing. I saw friends from a distance, walking towards the bus stop. One of them, well dressed as usual, tall, a little worried, a small briefcase in his hand, walked in the shadow of a stone wall. I was going to call out to him, but I didn't want to break my mood.

By one of the fruit stalls someone had turned over a box of blueberries, foggy grey blue. I bent down and picked one to eat. I bumped into a young man and apologised. He grabbed his friend's arm, looked at me, and I understood that he wanted to scare me, take my money, hit me. But I had come out without any money. I had just walked out. And suddenly the pain in my abdomen, the consciousness of my liver, was back. If he were to hit me in the stomach, I would lose consciousness from the pain. I said, 'I am ill. Very ill,' and touched his hand. He seemed offended, pulled away from me looking at his hand with a disgusted expression.

I walked home along the quay, passing the fishing boats. The mood was broken. To walk home was also to walk back into reality.

K has come from Jerusalem to take care of me. One evening we watched Sorrentino's *The Hand of God* on Netflix. After a while I asked her to pause it and shuffled off to the loo. When I stepped into the bathroom, I was struck by the realisation that I am ill – a second of vertigo, fear and helplessness. The film had made me forget my state, and I realised how terrible it is to forget. Distraction is good, denial is not. Not that this was denial, I just forgot for a while, and that hurt me. I want to be aware of my situation the whole time. Not to always talk about it or think about it, but to be within it. It's not an easy place to be, but it's the safest place for me right now.

Simon has sent flowers, Coppola's *Marie Antoinette*, pastilles, cake, underskirts, powder and eye shadow, an extravagance of things. Flowers I don't even know the names of except lilac and something else resembling an artichoke.

I want to write more but I can't. If it were morning, but it's almost nine in the evening. Tiredness has the same colour as peat. The same consistency. Sleep is more solid. It is both the stone thrown into the sea and the sea.

K gets takeaway and fruit, tidies the flat, takes care of me, goes through T's French homework with her. I get breathless from being up and mostly stay in bed. If I lie down I can think, breathe and speak better. T sleeps in my bed. She picks clothes for school and puts them in a pile on the floor so she doesn't have to wake K in the mornings.

In my dream about S the other night we made a film, which we also acted in. We were on a road in the country, walking arm in arm, and met ourselves as old – wearing the same clothes and walking at the same pace, quickly passing each other by. 'But is it drama or comedy?' I asked. She answered: 'Just play with it.'

The days pass by. I am happy about my thoughts, my notes, the plan for the new short story collection and the other book, the most important one, which is this one.

March 30th, 2022. I don't want to take a taxi to Karolinska hospital. I want to meet the building from the right direction, the right angle. Then it's mine. I met Jakob at the Gamla Stan underground station, travelled to St Eriksplan, and took the bus from there.

However slowly he walked, he still walked too fast.

I think about the entrance hall as a yard of light, the sun streaming in, but it's all artificial. The light, the space, is still calming. Like a transit hall. We love transit halls. The anonymity, the people, all on their way somewhere. One knows nothing about them. The sense of peace in the flow, everything passing by.

The oncologist said there's nothing they can do about my liver. It is full of metastases, and I also have metastases on the pelvis, a large one on the right, and several small ones on the left. They are not recommending any treatment. I have maybe three months left. I texted Jakob and asked him to come in. I told him, we held each other's hands tightly. A hard grip. We talked about palliative care at home. And about what my death will hopefully be like: I will gradually lose energy, become listless, introverted, and then fall asleep. That all sounds fine, except possibly the listlessness. We talked about my liver giving up, and about the whole system which is under such severe strain. My heart, which already now pulses fist-like in my chest, the pulse in my stomach kicking as T did before she was born. We talked about help for T. My oncologist wrote a prescription for cortisone to reduce the swelling in my abdomen, and a referral to the oncological therapist for T, me and my ex-husband.

We walked back across the light yard. Jakob bought me juice and a cheese sandwich. We didn't want to go. If we stayed, it would be as if nothing had happened. Outside, in the bright morning light, everything would become real. I rang those closest to me and cried. On the bus home we sat with our knees angled towards each other. A small child cried; an old man muttered to himself. There was so much light everywhere. I was so sad. I thought about T. That I will not see her grow up. Not know who she will become. Not see her children. To be near her . . . Her forehead, her neck, her large, bright eyes, her mouth, her soft cheeks. And then the consolation that I am the one who is going to die, not her. And when I'm dead I won't miss her any more.

She will remember me. She will carry my love inside her. She is thirteen, much too young. But old enough to not forget. Old enough to know what inside her is me, and us. And she is surrounded by love.

Jakob came into the oncologist's room and we looked at each other. His eyes are the same eyes as when he was little. There is something there which is like contained pain. He is my little brother. I said: 'I think I am going to die soon.'

In the evening T's brother came and went through her homework about space, the earth's rotational axis, the universe. They went to pick up some Thai takeaway. I fell asleep for a while on the bed. T removed her make-up and came to lie down, resting her head on my arm for a while. Her scent, her own, cutting through the smells of perfume and deodorant. It's like insanity and the elixir of life all at once. She will never understand how strong it is. When she has a child of her own she will feel that intoxication and not know that that was how I felt about her.

I woke up at dawn. Felt her calm breaths against mine, heard the black-headed gulls. I thought: this is everything.

I would like to tell the story of how beautiful it is, life. Of the sky, the birds. The light against the eyelids. But also of how it never quite allows itself to be described, and that it doesn't matter.

THE END

AFTERWORD

In late March 2022 Johanna got a second opinion from a specialist in London, on Zoom. I was there. He confirmed the Swedish prognosis, advised her to eat what she liked and added that she might feel sad, or angry, or think *why me*. Johanna, as I knew she would, found that irresistibly funny.

'Well,' she said ironically, laughing at the screen. 'Why *not* me?'

I went to Stockholm to help.

Time slowed down. Within a few days Johanna was more or less confined to bed and ate only the tiniest portions of foods she craved or could bear to think about.

A spoonful of semolina porridge with cinnamon and sugar, a slice of strawberry and a slice of banana.

A Japanese rice cracker with a sliver of avocado.

A wafer.

I made notes during the hospice team visits, making

sure I got the spelling and exact doses of the palliative medicines right. Johanna, already on morphine, cared not at all, fishing vaguely in the cotton shoe bag where she kept all her medication. She was right, of course – none of it really mattered very much at this stage. The team talked about Johanna's *goals*, and Johanna, being Johanna, immediately started talking about this book. I was anxious that they might skimp on the morphine if they thought her priority was a clear mind, so I prompted Johanna to say the next sentence, which I made a note of in case we needed a record: 'Johanna explained that her goal was not to prolong life for as long as possible, but to be able to die without pain, preferably in hospice.'

I held her warm, dry hand under the blanket. She squeezed my hand and I was overwhelmed by tears, shaking with suppressed sobs.

The days passed. Johanna slept and I sat by the window. Sounds drifted up – voices, steps, the bark of a dog. H, Johanna's psychoanalyst, came for a visit. He stayed with Johanna a while and came out weeping. We wept, together.

Johanna's voice turned weak and hoarse. At times she knelt on the bed, eyes closed, leaning forwards on cushions and pillows to alleviate the pain of the tumours, hard masses under the stretched skin of her abdomen.

She sipped water and sucked on ice or frozen Coca-Cola, a cold cloth on her forehead.

She had a morphine pump attached to one arm and a port on the other where we could inject top-up morphine, liquid against nausea and tranquillisers. The syringes – three of each medicine, plus salty water to flush the line – were neatly lined up on a tray.

I cried again and again and was comforted by the very person whose imminent disappearance I was grieving. She held my arm and smiled; she leant back and closed her eyes, we sat in grief, in communion.

Did our grief comfort her or burden her? I don't know.

I heard her voice when she was silent. I heard her footsteps when she was sleeping.

I'll always be there, she whispered when I told her I'd heard her.

I read the newspapers as she slept and the meaning escaped me. Sentences made no sense, I read them over and over.

Johanna slept; so pale. She was increasingly absent. But every once in a while, she would come back – an ironic lifting of the eyebrow, some comment, something complicit between us.

I took out the rubbish and a Roma woman on the street giving out bunches of miniature daffodils asked for the returns. I gave her the empty bottles and she thanked me in her broken Swedish and stored them neatly by her feet. That evening the huge plastic sheeting on the community centre on the square ripped and whipped in the wind, loud and peremptory against the relentless grey sky. Falling asleep I saw in my mind's eye a tickertape of graffiti on old buildings, walls covered in words, black, red, all sizes; snatches of Swedish I had heard, words on the street and in shops, words flying through the ether and attaching themselves to walls.

April 12th, Ersta hospice. I sat in the chair by Johanna's bed, waiting and watching. Her breaths were slow and uneven. Sometimes she missed one.

She woke up. I gave her some water and her teeth crashed on the hard glass. The nurse brought a straw, but Johanna did not have the energy to suck so she got a plastic cup with a spout; I filled it with ice and a little water.

The morphine made her faint. 'Like falling backwards into blackness,' she said.

So many good drugs in the world; so few in that grim room.

T came to visit with Tomas and his other daughter. I found a sunny terrace with a sliver of a view of the bay and stood there for a while, propping the heavy door open with a stone. Tomas texted me, Johanna wanted something, but they couldn't understand what. It was water, she always wanted water, icy water from the plastic cup, sips almost too tiny to swallow.

I sat by Johanna's bed that night, counting the seconds during the intervals between her laboured breaths. She slept or was unconscious. Sometimes I looked out over the inner courtyard of the hospital. The windows across the yard were dark except one, a room diagonally across where I could see a mysterious golden mask hanging on a wall.

K slept on the fold-out daybed behind me. I brought my chair closer to the hospital bed. Johanna was restless and sometimes threw her arms up. Earlier that day she had sometimes held the plastic cup, hands white and trembling, blue veins on white skin. Now she could hold nothing. She made sounds, moaning, with half-closed eyes. A nurse gave her top-up morphine.

Four hours later, at one in the morning, I asked for more morphine. There were two nurses at the station, a man and a woman. They looked at each other, then the man got up to give her another top-up. A double top-up.

There was some kind of palpable communication between them before he got up.

A pause.

The window was open, Johanna had complained about being too hot. I sat with a blanket. K slept, still, on the daybed behind me.

At 4 a.m. Johanna's breathing seemed calmer. I thought she would survive for another day, perhaps another few days. K woke up and I said I would go home to get some sleep. I got a taxi, then found myself locked out of my hotel until the driver of the baker's van woke the night porter, who let me in. *Sleep well*, he said pointedly as I walked towards the lift.

Two and a half hours later Johanna passed away.

Someone called and I went back to Ersta, walking into the room despite the sign, *family only*. Johanna's father was there, and her brother. I briefly put my hand on Johanna's head. Her cheek was icy-cold, colder, it seemed, than anything else in the room.

She was lying under my blanket. The nurses had tidied the room, those routine activities, and had also done what most of us never have to do: prepare a dead body.

I found K in the day room and she told me what had happened – about falling asleep again and waking up to the sound of calmer breathing. She sat with Johanna, who was still unconscious, speaking to her, stroking her arm.

The intervals between the breaths were uneven.

And then the breathing stopped.

Death is both abstract and concrete. The abstract quality (consciousness, a soul) disappears, the concrete body remains.

A corpse.

Johanna's body at Ersta was like an intricately detailed machine or a work of art. The enormous complexity of the body, all systems off.

A great silence.

Thoughts, images, sounds, heat, movement, electricity – all gone. Johanna's short, clean hair bounced under my hand. Her eyes were closed; she smiled her faintly ironic smile.

Later K and I went back to Johanna's flat. We tidied up a bit. The terrible thing that had happened felt like a stranglehold round the neck, a weight in the chest. There were dustballs under the radiators, we heard voices from the street. Everything was normal, if by *normal* you mean the constant backdrop to unfolding illness.

There was the wall of bookcases behind the big writing table. Johanna's artworks on the wall, shoes and coats on the stand by the front door. The door to T's room was open, the bed unmade. The only thing we talked about removing before T came back with her dad to pack her things was a plastic commode, not used, which the hospice team had dropped off.

A big white cube. It reminded me of the tumours.

A memory. A few days before Johanna died, I stepped into the lift. A man came in after me and cheerfully introduced himself. He had just moved in, he said, and would like to meet the neighbours. I don't remember what I said or what he answered, but he understood that someone was ill, maybe dying. We stood in silence for a few seconds as the old lift slowly ascended.

There was a glass wall between the life in Johanna's flat and the life in the building. People came and went, moved in and moved out and a woman lay dying on the third floor.

The last email I received from Johanna was dated April 9th, four days before she died:

I also long [to find] my way back to the time that was. The mornings in the country, dawn light, my grandmother's silence. We were like roe deer. We were like things we knew nothing about. I think so often about sleeping animals and human bodies, how we make our nests. This summer I pointed out places where animals had slept in the dry grass. I could see the animals in my mind's eye. The contours of them were still there in the high morning air. Muscles, sinews under soft fur. The movement of the ears, the animal preparing, finding its bearing. The nerves, scents. Memories or dreams? The landscape, the silence, but also the sudden loud noise of the sea, light and dark possessing me. It flowed through my body until it was saturated. Something started in me then. Several things. A great sense of joy and calm. Those places of flattened grass were presence itself. To be so full of beginnings, caves, canals, open spaces.

To long to find one's way back in time. To search for something but also to long for it. To yearn but also to wait.

The email was a painstaking transcript of something she had written earlier, by hand. It was meant to be part of the book.

Let it stand as that.

Months later. Johanna's notebooks are on my desk. I see a buzzard mirrored in the pond behind the barn where I write. Three deer pass by the trees on the other side and wade through shallow water to the little island. They stand quite still, until one of them snorts and shakes its head; they are there a little longer, then they move on.

A hornet bounces on the open window.

The walls became the world all around.

I suppose the blue chair is in some other room now.

Johanna's flat is sold. Strangers will be looking at the tree outside the flat. They too might notice patterns on the roof opposite. See the magpie and the clouds, listen to the voices from the street, open and close the fridge.

All time is now. It's summer, 2002. Johanna and I are drinking white wine tasting of water and dancing to Paolo Conte in my kitchen in London.

> *Via via*
> *Vieni via di qui*
> . . .
> *It's wonderful*
> *It's wonderful*
> *It's wonderful*
> *Good luck my baby*
> *It's wonderful*
> *It's wonderful*
> *It's wonderful*
> *I dream of you*

I am writing my speech for her memorial; she is a palpable presence, a ghost, next to me. I read her what I have written. 'It's wonderful,' she says, with that indefinable expression on her face which means she is about to object, '. . . but aren't you going to talk about my books? I think I miss my identity as a writer in this context.'

'But Sofia and Tobias will talk about that,' I say. 'I am talking about you as my friend. My best friend in life.'

'Yes, true!' she says. She holds my arm, we are crying; now she is in her bed, now she is dying.

And so it goes.

So it goes.

Acknowledgements

I thank my husband, Eric Abraham, for steadfast support (and a thousand games of chess and Scrabble) in the course of editing and translating this book.

To Johanna's brother, Jakob Wästberg, his wife, Helene Stevenberg, and all the people who helped to take care of Johanna, especially Karin Ekblom, Sofia Wiberg, Tobias Theorell, Tomas Lappalainen and Henry Jablonski: a huge thank you.

Thank you to everyone at Albert Bonniers and Granta who helped make this book a reality, especially Linden Lawson, Christine Lo, Patty Rennie, Isabella Depiazzi, Daniela Silva, Bella Lacey, Lotta Aquilonius, Albert Bonnier, Anna-Karin Korpi-Öhlund. Thank you also to my agent, Sarah Chalfant, for moral support and encouragement.

Thank you, finally, to my son, Daniel Hotz, who was with me in Stockholm when Johanna was dying; consoled me when I was inconsolable, fed me when I didn't know I was hungry, and made the unbearable bearable through countless acts of kindness.

This book is dedicated to T, Johanna's beloved daughter.